Hilary Minns is edi
National Association
primary school
West Midlands, where an

In *Read It To Me Now!* Hilary Minns examines and describes the
progress of Gurdeep, Gemma, Anthony, Geeta and Reid as they
to read in primary school. Her conclusions – strengthened by a richly
diverse discussion of theories about reading and language – suggest that
since each child takes their first steps towards reading as part of their
family and cultural tradition, schools need a theory and practice of
literacy whose foundations are set in an understanding of children's
own real world of experience – their own lived lives.

Also in the Virago Education Series
In association with the University of London Institute of
Education

*Wasting Girls' Time: The History and Politics of Home
Economics*
Dena Attar

Un/Popular Fictions
Gemma Moss

Teaching Black Literature
Suzanne Scafe

Counting Girls Out
The Girls and Mathematics Unit, Institute of Education
Compiled by Valerie Walkerdine

Read It To Me Now!

Learning at Home and at School

Hilary Minns

Published by VIRAGO PRESS Limited 1990
20–23 Mandela Street, Camden Town, London NW1 0HQ

A CIP Catalogue record for this book
is available from the British Library

Typeset in Great Britain by Burns & Smith Ltd, Derby

Printed by Cox & Wyman Ltd, Reading, Berkshire

For Anthony, Geeta, Gemma, Gurdeep and Reid

If the culture of the teacher is to become part of the consciousness of the child, then the culture of the child must first be in the consciousness of the teacher. (Basil Bernstein, 1970)

CONTENTS

Acknowledgements

My thanks are due particularly to Gemma, Gurdeep, Anthony, Reid and Geeta and to each of their families for giving me their time and their trust, and allowing me to be with them and to learn from them. I also need to remember John Baker, Bill Thompson, Mr and Mrs Bridle and the late Terry McPhilimey, who all helped me to understand more about the Courthouse Green area as it has developed and changed over the last sixty years. My thanks too to Angela Webb and Beryl Glasscoe, the children's teachers during their first school year, who spent time talking with me, allowed me into their classrooms to observe the children and to 'borrow' them at odd times, and read drafts of their reading biographies. Thanks are also due to Sue Davis, Anne Baker and Mike Torbe, who read and commented on drafts of my original dissertation. I am grateful too to Tony Burgess for his advice and support and to Jane Miller for her encouragement and help.

I owe a particular debt of gratitude to Margaret Spencer, who encouraged me initially with this project. Over the years, through her writing and her lecturing, she has helped me to understand more about the reading process, and in particular to appreciate why children need stories and rhymes in their lives, to read and to grow on.

Introduction

When I was a primary teacher my central professional concern was with finding out more about language and learning, and my daily interaction in the classroom was one of enquiry into the learning that was taking place. I was fascinated, for instance, by the processes involved in learning to read and wanted to know more about what was happening to individual children in my class. Why did Natasha suddenly begin to read in her head one day, just like that? Why didn't Jamie choose to read, though I knew he could really? Why was that particular story so important for David? When would Zoe read something other than Enid Blyton? In the evenings, or at weekends or holiday times, I read books, articles, attended conferences or joined groups of teachers with the same concerns, and ideas were put forward, discussed, taken up, discarded.

The main ideas I embraced then – which continue to influence my thinking – were framed around the psycholinguistic theories of Frank Smith (1971) and Kenneth Goodman (1972). From Frank Smith I learned how to make the task of learning to read easier for children, helping them to make sense of what they read rather than insisting on accuracy. Kenneth Goodman's work showed me how to respond positively to the 'mistakes' of inexperienced readers, seeing these as 'miscues' or mismatches between the text and what was actually read, celebrating the reader's inventiveness and creativity and seeing their miscues as evidence of the vast amount of linguistic knowledge and experience they brought to the task of reading.

But now, some years later, I realise that I wasn't able to answer many important questions about reading to my satisfaction because although I tried to see each child as a full person, my ideas were framed solely around the child as individual learner; I thought that by focusing on one individual I could make comfortably universal generalisations about all learners irrespective of who they were, or of their backgrounds. I took no account of the collaborative manner in which children learned to read and write, even though it was happening in front of my eyes.

I saw no reason, either, to acknowledge the social and cultural contexts in which this language learning took place; the world of the children as I perceived it was my world of the classroom and what was important was what happened within the classroom; and though I knew the children's parents and spoke to them, sometimes at length, on parents' evenings, I never paid much attention to the kinds of knowledge and experiences of reading that were part of the life of the community beyond the school gates; not particularly because I wanted to hold myself away from it, but because I had no idea that by listening to and observing the way these families used a rich living language I would have a firmer base on which to begin to build a theory about the children's reading, a theory whose foundations were set in an understanding of their own real world of experience, their own lived lives.

Some years ago, the responsibility of a headship brought me into a different, less restricted relationship with a new school community and after spending time discovering my own role, getting to know people, in school and out, and learning about new sets of community values, my interest in language resurfaced and I wanted to formulate a school reading policy that reflected my concerns about learning to read. Coincidentally, I was urged to buy and read *Ways With Words* by Shirley Brice Heath (1983), and it was this book, with its exciting analysis of language and culture in two communities, that showed me a new way of looking at reading. Here, for example, Brice Heath describes a reading practice she observed in the Black working-class community she calls Trackton:

> Reading was a public group affair for almost all members of Trackton from the youngest to the oldest. Miss Lula sometimes read her Bible alone, and Annie Mae would sometimes quietly read magazines she brought home, but to read alone was frowned upon, and individuals who did so were accused of being anti-social. Aunt Berta had a son who as a child used to slip away from the cotton field and read under a tree. He is now a grown man with children, and he has obtained a college degree, but the community still tells tales about his peculiar boyhood habits of wanting to go off and read alone. (p.191)

The images of those people reading in Trackton have remained with me to this day, along with many others from the book. I'd never read obser-

vations about reading like these before and they excited me. I knew that
if I wanted to learn more about the children and their reading in my own
school, I needed to get out into the community in order to begin to make
sense of the world the children were living in, and to focus on the ways
their families used reading and writing in their own lives. Without this
basic understanding I knew it wouldn't be possible for me to learn more
about patterns of reading. This gave me a fascinating area for study and
prompted me to invite six families to work with me to help me observe
and record their four-year-olds learning to become readers during the year
when they moved from home into school. This book has grown out of
the research I did with five of these families for an MA dissertation in
1987. It is for people who are interested in the reading experiences of
their own young child, those responsible for a group of learners at school
and those who want to see a sense of community developing from learning at home and at school. The 'adult experienced reader' I refer to in
the later chapters encompasses all those who have a responsibility for supporting a young child who is learning to read.

Each of the first five chapters tells the story of a four-year-old child:
Gurdeep, Gemma, Anthony, Geeta and Reid, as they learn to become
readers. We meet them first in their homes three months before they
come to school to look at the kinds of reading experiences they have,
then we follow them into their classrooms to see them learning to read
with their teachers. As we observe the children, two things become clear:
first, they had all taken their first steps towards becoming readers before
they came to school, either by observing, or being part of, the reading
and writing activities of their home and neighbourhood; secondly, each
child's reading experience is markedly different because it is influenced
and supported by their family's social and cultural traditions. These themes
are explored again in later chapters.

Chapter 6 shows how the children are developing positive views of
themselves as readers; although they are still inexperienced in many ways
they are getting a feel for reading by using the print they see around them
in the community, recognising some words and memorising some lines
of stories and poems, developing a sense of literary language and learning
about the conventions of a book.

Chapter 7 explores the importance of story and literature in the children's
lives and in the process of learning to read. It shows how the children's

world of make-believe play is extended and enriched by the imaginative world they enter through the world of the story.

Chapter 8 describes the nature of the delicate one-to-one relationship between the young child reader and the supporting adult, whether parent or teacher. Typically, the adult sets up the situation for the reading, stresses enjoyment and understanding, is responsible for reading all or most of the story, and encourages the child to respond through conversation.

Chapter 9 examines the way in which the children's learning is enmeshed in the social and cultural traditions of each child's family and community, and the implications this has for teachers, parents and children. It suggests ways of helping schools and communities to set up a total literacy environment for children that takes account of the views of parents, teachers and children and embraces learning in the home, the community and the school. The book ends with short pieces about Gurdeep, Gemma, Anthony, Geeta and Reid describing their reading lives three years after this study began.

But before we meet these five children I need to say a little about the way their teachers help them learn to read, and to put this in its historical perspective. It is important to do this because theories about learning to read change and develop as fresh insights are made and translated into classroom practice.

In the children's school, learning to read is an informal and gradual process and children are helped to develop reading rules themselves, with the support of their teachers. When they share a book with their teacher they are expected to relate it to their own experience and to take over the reading when they feel they can, though no attempt is made to make them read the actual words in the book unless they wish to. They are encouraged to read with older children and children in their own class, so that they become each other's teachers. Gradually, as they become more experienced, they begin to rely on less support from an adult until finally they become independent readers.

This brief description of reading practice is based on a set of beliefs stemming from the psycholinguistic theories of the 1970s to which I referred earlier. These were given prominence by people like Kenneth Goodman, and Frank Smith, who summarises the process like this:

> Children learn to read only by reading. Therefore, the only way to facilitate their learning to read is to make reading easy for them. This means continuously

making critical and insightful decisions – not forcing children to read for words when they are, or should be, reading for meaning; not forcing them to slow down when they should speed up; not requiring caution when they should be taking chances; not worrying about speech when the topic is reading; not discouraging errors. (1984, p.23)

This theory of reading has changed practice in many primary schools and profoundly influenced teachers who want to help children to look for meaning in their reading. When I was a student at training college in the 1960s I knew nothing of Frank Smith or Kenneth Goodman and I was expected to teach children to read using basal readers or reading scheme books, which are specially constructed, often by educational psychologists, to help children read using a step-by-step approach. Reading skills are arranged in a hierarchical structure: letter by letter, word by word, line by line, sentence by sentence, page by page and book by book. The language is carefully controlled and there is a great deal of repetition of words which have to be recognised and remembered. This repetition is reinforced using 'flashcards' and tested on word-recognition tests.

Twenty-three years ago, when Reid's teacher began teaching at the same school, her headteacher told her that the reception children in her class had to know the twenty-six letter-sounds by the end of their first term in school, and should have read the first yellow *Janet and John* basal reader perfectly by Christmas. In response to this pressure, she stayed behind after school each evening and heard children read as late as five o'clock. Their parents 'would leave them as long as I could stay', she said. Interestingly, this wasn't the way she'd learned to read herself. 'My dad taught me', she remembers. 'He used to read to me for hours. I nearly always had an adult to read with, grandmother or auntie. I could read before I went to school and I could write a bit as well.' Like many other teachers, she set this experience aside and took over the professional view of teaching reading which she learned at training college, just as I did. Over the years *Janet and John* readers and the *Beacon* readers were replaced by other basal readers, *Kathy and Mark* and *Ginn 360*. The tradition of keeping children at school to read to their teacher had long since ended, but children were still encouraged to learn to read by recognising individual words, and they took word tins home containing new words for their parents to help them learn – a common practice in infant schools, and an interesting forerunner of the home-school learning policies that have been in the forefront of educational thinking in community education in Coventry since the 1970s, documented by Widlake and Macleod (1984).

This way of teaching reading was based on behaviourist theories of learning, where the reading process was broken down into manageable parts, each mastered separately. It was meant to simplify the process of learning to read by presenting reading to children in small steps. Tansley (1967) summarises this approach:

> A good reading programme consists of four parts: the development of readiness; the acquisition of a sight vocabulary of words which occur frequently in children's reading and spoken vocabulary; the development of independent reading by the use of phonic analysis and synthesis and other word recognition techniques; the development of speedy, relaxed silent reading for content, ideas and pleasure. (p.28)

But what this approach actually did was to make the process more difficult for children. They could not use meaning to help them understand what they were reading because they were denied chunks of meaning in the form of a story, or even of a sentence. And when they were given a book to read its language was so artificial, its subject matter so minimal and its illustrations of such poor quality as to make it scarcely worth the trouble reading: it could hardly be otherwise given the constraints of the reading programme. Children were denied an emotional response because there was nothing in the book to respond to and they were not given the support of good literary language.

So it seems almost inevitable that as the psycholinguistic theories were gaining support in schools, there was a move away from basal readers towards the kind of book that children could respond to by drawing on their own experiences, bringing their intelligence and emotional awareness to reading. In the 1970s Margaret Spencer's work on the importance of story (1976) helped to persuade teachers of their centrality in the curriculum; her work has been given practical emphasis by Jill Bennett (1979) and more recently by Liz Waterland (1988).

The result of this is that Gurdeep, Geeta, Anthony, Reid and Gemma will find that traditional tales and picture-story books form the basis of their classroom libraries. They will listen to a story read or told by their teacher at least once a day and have access to book boxes containing four copies of the same picture-story book and its accompanying tape which they can listen to on headphones in the classroom. Sometimes the teacher will set up conditions of silence as she invites a child to become the reader of a book for the whole class, thus creating feelings of worth and self-esteem as she hands over a book to be retold by a child. The children will be encouraged to tell stories of their own lives too, or stories they've made up. Some of these will be dictated and written up into books.

The children will be given books to read and share that offer them fun, excitement and challenge, right from the start. Teachers choose books that are skilfully and elegantly written by people who know how well young children use their imaginations to understand and become part of the storyworld created by the writers. They are books that invite children to become readers in the sense that they tell a story, have a strong authorial voice, contain illustrations that can be explored and interrogated alongside the words in order to make sense of the story, and give children reading lessons about the way a book works. In addition to these stories, other books will find their way into the classrooms. These range from the books children bring from home to read at school to those made by the children themselves, or by teachers or older children in the school.

I have concentrated my attention on the school's view of reading, rather than on the reading and writing that happens every day in the children's homes, partly to show what the children can expect when they come to school but also because the theories of reading I have outlined so far make no reference to the social and cultural contexts in which the children's learning takes place. However, we know now from the work of ethnographers like Shirley Brice Heath (1983) and Marilyn Cochran-Smith (1986) that children's learning can be fully understood only within a framework that acknowledges their lives at home and in their communities. It is necessary now to look afresh at our present knowledge of the reading process to find ways of incorporating children's reading experiences learned at home into school policy, so that a total literacy environment can be achieved.

The National Curriculum for English gives us scope for doing this by acknowledging that children bring experiences of language and literacy to school with them. The programmes of study make it clear that links need to be forged between home and school experience to help a child to become a confident language user in a variety of situations. We are told, for instance: 'Reading activities should build on the oral language and experiences which pupils bring from home.' And: 'Teachers should take account of the important link between home and school, actively encouraging parents to participate and share in their child's reading.'

There is welcome acknowledgement, too, of the variety of written language in children's homes and its importance in early literacy:

> Pupils will have seen different kinds of writing in the home – their names on birthday cards or letters, forms, shopping lists and so on. Those whose parents are literate in a language other than English may have observed writing in their own first language, for which there may be a different writing system.

There is plenty here to be pleased about, though the respect for bilingualism still needs to be accommodated in the attainment targets and programmes of study. The National Curriculum supports our knowledge that children do not arrive at school illiterate; that each one brings to school with them their own unique identity as a language user and their own particular reading experiences learned within their families and communities. This study has grown out of my own need to know more about the importance of this and more about children like Gemma, Gurdeep, Reid, Anthony and Geeta.

When I was a classroom teacher I came to believe that the kinds of questions I asked about learning should enable me to look at each child as a separate human being. They should be questions that allowed each of us to retain our humanity and dignity. I wanted this study to share those same qualities, seen in the context of the school community, and to help me towards an enriched understanding of other people's lives in a way that was celebratory, giving them strength and dignity and allowing me to feel comfortable and honest in my observations and intuitions. I was influenced by the kinds of beliefs about human nature I met in the writing of people like Brian Jackson and George Eliot – who, incidentally, lived in Nuneaton and then in Coventry, just a mile or two from the children's school, for the first thirty years of her life. In 'Janet's Repentance' she writes:

> ... surely the only true knowledge of our fellow-man is that which enables us to feel with him, – which gives us a fine ear for the heart-pulses that are beating under the mere clothes of circumstance and opinion. Our subtlest analysis of schools and sects must miss the essential truth, unless it be lit up by the love that sees in all forms of human thought and work, the life and death struggles of separate human beings. (p.322)

I initially wanted to find a way of working with the whole school community, but was quickly persuaded that this was going to have to be a modest study, fitted in somehow around a full-time job. I read, and enjoyed, Brian Jackson's *Starting School* (1979) and thought there was a possibility of working with six children and their families as he did, but with my central focus on the children's reading. I wanted to work with six children and their families who between them reflected the ethnic and sociocultural diversity of our school: two Afro-Caribbean, two Asian and two white children. A boy and girl from each grouping gave me a gender dimension. (The Afro-Caribbean girl in fact left the country shortly after I began work on the research and she is therefore omitted from the study.)

In the end I chose two white children, a boy and a girl called Reid and Gemma; Gurdeep and Geeta were choices because they were Sikhs and their families formed part of our largest minority group within the school; I selected Anthony since he was the only Afro-Caribbean boy to be admitted to school that year. In addition, I already knew the children's parents a little, since they had older brothers and sisters in the school, and this made my initial contact easier.

First of all I asked each family if they would be willing to help me undertake a study about their child becoming a reader. I told them I felt that as teachers we needed to know much more about the kinds of reading children saw around them and joined in with at home, and that it was increasingly important for us to understand more about the way parents helped children learn to read both before they came to school and when they were at school. I explained that the study would involve me coming to talk with them on various occasions, and monitoring their child in school. They agreed to my proposal. I also spoke to the two teachers who would be working with these children over the year, and they agreed to help me too.

At this point I didn't have a set of questions in my head, contrary to normal models of research. Instead, I trusted that questions and hypotheses would emerge as I got deeper into the task of exploring five beginning readers and understanding more about the social and cultural dimensions of the reading process. Looking back, though, I recognise that two basic assumptions lay behind my research into learning to read at home and at school. First, since all five children are part of a print culture, I guessed they would have seen print around them in some degree before they came to school, irrespective of the amount of reading and writing in the home. Secondly, I knew that each child in my study would have to find a way of making sense of the kinds of reading and writing that were part of home life and school life.

I visited each family on three separate occasions and interviewed them about their child, their social practices, and their views of literacy. Sometimes I saw only the mother, sometimes both parents; often the child was there together with older brothers and sisters, who joined in the conversations too. I tape-recorded the interviews. Then I asked each parent to tape-record themselves reading with their child, sharing a book they both liked. Finally, I asked each family to list for me all the kinds of written material they used and saw around them in their home.

After that, in school, I observed the children in class when I could. Occasionally I set aside specific times to visit their classroom, but more often I would go to observe them, or talk with them individually, when I had a spare half-hour or so, and I believe my examples are representative of characteristic interactions over the year. Sometimes I listened to the children reading and, with their permission, tape-recorded the sessions. I also recorded them reading with their teachers and with their peers. I collected samples of their early writing. After school, or in holiday times, I talked with their teachers to discuss their progress and also visited their parents twice or three times over the year to keep in touch.

Throughout I tried to be observer, listener, sharer, interpreter and finally storyteller of events in the lives of these children and their families. I have never, though, pretended any kind of neutrality; indeed, my own interests, previous teaching experiences and intuition will already have been apparent in my choice of study and the way I've decided to define it. It will be there again in the five stories, informing my choice of what to record, select and omit from the evidence. I recognise too that my position as the children's headteacher placed me as an authority figure in relation to the children and their families and distanced me from them, even though they were seeing me in a different role: that of information-gatherer in their homes, drawing on their knowledge and experience. Perhaps too the families took up a dual stance towards me: that of traditional parent, a little awed to have the headteacher call round, and that of the secure possessor of knowledge I found valuable. I enjoyed getting closer to them than I've ever been to other families – eating with them, watching television, talking and sharing ideas.

By the end of the children's second term in school I had amassed a great deal of evidence and needed to find a way of presenting it that reflected and illuminated the children's lives and their entrance into reading. Each child's life was uniquely rich and I chose to become a biographer for each of them, writing each story as it unfolded in its own way, and asking the parents to read and comment as I went along. By the time each was written I wanted to have five personal histories in front of me. I guessed they would look more like literature than scientific research because, like literature, they would deal with human issues by telling a precise story. Any universal truths would come out of the particularities of each story, as in a novel. What follows, then, is a glimpse into the living and reading worlds of these five young children.

A Note on Transcribing

In making the transcripts I have used the following signs:

' '   to indicate where the actual text of a book is being read

...   to indicate a pause

–   to indicate a sudden break in utterance because of interruption

.   to indicate (as far as it is possible to judge from talk) the end of a sentence

words in italics to indicate where two people are speaking at the same time

PART ONE

Five Children

Introduction: The Neighbourhood and the School

The north-east of Coventry, where the school lies and where the families of Geeta, Gemma, Gurdeep, Reid and Anthony live, is an area of about eight square miles, fringed by the M6 Motorway and giving way to fields beyond it. The area is bisected by a main road, busy with traffic commuting to and from the motorway and outlying areas, and on either side of this main road are rows of streets of uniform council housing, mainly terraced, with gardens front and rear. Much of this is in the process of being modernised and families are moved out for about twelve weeks while work is carried out to give them indoor lavatories and central heating, though some have opted to buy their council houses. Further into the city the houses are older and form dark blocks of terraces, with no front gardens.

The area has undergone massive changes in the last sixty years. Before the Morris car works and Alfred Herbert Machine Tools brought industrial development on a large scale, much of the north-east was farmland, and small communities of close-knit families lived in villages or scatterings of houses along the main road and beyond, linked by names which still remain today in local districts of Coventry: Courthouse Green, Bell Green, Alderman's Green, Hall Green, Wyken Green, Henley Green, Potter's Green. Families eked out a living by working as agricultural labourers on the farms, and supplemented their wages by keeping chickens and pigs, while the women took in washing. A few of these families remain and every so often there are other reminders of the past: weavers' cottages dating from the eighteenth century and street names like Shuttle Street, Weaver's Walk and Heddle Grove testify to the involvement with weaving in the area. But Workhouse Lane has been replaced by Profitt Avenue, and stuccoed council houses line each side of the road. A new brick

Hindu temple has been built on the corner: 'They shouldn't have built it there,' a ten-year-old white boy tells me, as we stand looking at the temple together. 'They bring all their cars and park them down our road. The boy next door lets their tyres down!' An indication that racial hostility still exists in the area.

The 1920s and 1930s saw the first real industrial expansion as the Morris and Herbert works brought families into the area. 'You got all your skilled workers this side of town,' says Bill Thompson, a retired Morris worker. He adds:

> The Morris was known as 'The Mint' and when I was twenty-two I was getting ten guineas a week. There was money to burn around here. Nobody was out of work. You got more money at the Morris than any other factory in England. When I was fifteen I was earning three times as much as my father. It didn't matter what age you was, if you earned it you had it. The sky was the limit.

Soon, most of the farmland was being sold for redevelopment to house the workers and their families. The 1960s were still times of full employment and the north-east responded by building more houses, two blocks of high-rise flats and a shopping precinct.

Full employment continued a long tradition of immigration into Coventry, including my own, attracting people from all over Britain and from the Indian subcontinent and the West Indies too. Alfred Herbert's employed men from India in their foundry while Afro-Caribbean men worked at the Morris factory and their wives became nurses. Some Asian families bought corner shops in the area or, like Geeta's parents, set up clothing factories or other family-run businesses.

But those with jobs are the lucky ones, and when I began this study in 1986 it was clear that for many the boom time was over and industry in Coventry was in decline. Unemployment has brought in its train stress, poverty and unhappiness and old people who remember the area as it was fifty years ago will tell you that as a consequence standards have fallen. They testify to the plight of the old people – white, Afro-Caribbean and Asian – who live alone in the high-rise blocks of flats and are afraid to go out at night. They talk about the increasing muggings, vandalism, graffiti, drug abuse, underage drinking and theft; they despair of one-parent families and speak longingly of a return to a former lifestyle, where you took your cap off to greet a lady or the parson and watched as the Church

Lads' Brigade marched around the streets on the first Sunday of each month.

The school, built in the 1950s on former farmland to educate the growing population, is set back from the road. It's a stark, sprawling building, standing flat-roofed and inelegant in grounds of mature trees and playing fields: a kind of oasis in a desert of bleak houses. Inside, fifteen classrooms lead off from long corridors. Two of these classrooms are for reception children, and it's into these rooms that Gurdeep, Geeta, Gemma, Anthony and Reid will go on their first day at school. We will follow them.

1

Gurdeep[1]

It was Gurdeep's first day at school. He was four years and four months old and his mother had dressed him with care, tying his hair in a topknot which was covered with a small handkerchief. She held his hand as she brought him to the classroom, and in the other hand she carried a box containing his sandwiches for dinner time. There was a space picture on the box, and a word in large red capitals was emblazoned across the picture: 'Transformers!' Gurdeep would tell me excitedly as he ate his dinner a few weeks later, perhaps recognising that the word was the same as the one on his toys at home and on the television advertisements he watched.

Gurdeep was greeted by his teacher and shown where to hang his bag and jacket. Above his peg she had printed 'Gurdeep', and she pointed his name out to him. An early reading lesson; his first in school, perhaps. Then he sat down in the classroom with his mother and played with the Lego. Five more 'new' children were similarly greeted. Eight others, who had started school the previous week, were already making their way confidently around the room.

Normally at this time of the morning, before he started school, Gurdeep might be getting ready for nursery or, on the mornings he didn't go, playing with his Transformers or cars, or colouring or painting, watching television or talking in Punjabi with his grandmother. Now, as he looked around the classroom, he may have remembered some of the things that were there when he visited last July: the goldfish, the doll's house, the house corner, the carpet, shelves and books, a settee and a small red chair; plants and ornaments to look at and touch. Further round, a table with glue, paste and paints, and boxes for junk modelling. On the wall, some children's pictures with 'Look at our pictures' printed below; opposite, a blackboard with nothing written on it, and a noticeboard with typed notices and timetables pinned up. And a shelf with jigsaws. Perhaps these reminded Gurdeep of the ones he enjoyed doing at home, and certainly in a few weeks he would become expert at making The Ship and The Little Red Hen, sitting cross-legged on the carpet in silent concentration.

The clock showed that it was nearly ten o'clock, and Gurdeep's mother got ready to go. Gurdeep waved to her as she left. He was used to saying goodbye to her for a few hours; she had brought him to the nursery annexe further up the corridor for the whole of the previous year. Today, though, would be the first time he had eaten his dinner away from her.

Gurdeep's mother has the same feelings now as she walks down the corridor as she had four years ago when she first brought her daughter, Tejinder, to school; there's a sense of pride in bringing her son to school for the first time, meeting the teacher and seeing what will happen in the classroom. She has always been interested in the ways the school will help her children to be educated. Every night from now on, when she collects her two children, she will ask the teachers, 'Are they behaving?' 'Are they taking an interest?' 'Do they need some help at home?'

I already know Gurdeep quite well, having spent time with his family in the final months before he started school, talking with them in their home over cups of cinnamon tea, eating meals together, accompanying them to the Sikh temple. Our discussions and my visits, and what I have seen, have enabled me to learn about the literacy events in Gurdeep's early life – those different literacies made available to him by his family and community. Gurdeep has been surrounded by several quite different literacy practices in his home ever since he was a baby. These practices are embedded in the set of institutions and relations that form his culture: the religious life of his family and community and the domestic life, work and leisure occupations of those around him. Gurdeep's parents have a conscious desire to prepare him for school and at the same time they want him to understand Sikh culture and beliefs. Gurdeep has been read to since he was very small. When he was a baby 'you'd be reading or writing and he'd be out there sitting in that corner and quickly he would pick it up'.

As Gurdeep's parents tell me this, I sit opposite them on an easy chair in the through lounge of their home. They sit on the settee and we drink tea, all of us tired after a day at work. There is a picture of the Golden Temple at Amritsar on the wall, together with brightly coloured por-

traits of the Sikh prophets. Gurdeep's father has just finished mowing
the lawn and the activity has made his hay fever worse. It's a warm June
evening, and he's taken off his jacket, shoes and socks. His dark red tur-
ban is bound neatly round his head. His wife looks cooler in her shulwar
kamiz. Tejinder and Gurdeep are drinking orange juice and colouring pictures at the table and their youngest brother, Navdeep, is in bed. We
talk about work and school, gardening and allergies, and then Gurdeep's
grandfather comes in. He is white-haired and speaks only a little English,
but he smiles and says hello to me. Gurdeep's mother covers her head
respectfully as he comes in the door. Later, I am invited to eat with the
family and we have a meal of vegetable curry and rice with salad. Tejinder takes her grandfather's meal to him and he eats it sitting on an
easy chair at the far end of the room. Grandmother sits at the table with
the rest of us and occasionally encourages Gurdeep to eat more quickly,
sometimes feeding him pieces of chapatti herself.

Gurdeep's mother tells me about her own mother, who lives in London. 'She's a good talker,' she says. 'She's a very cheerful person. She
tells us the stories about her past when she was a child. She tells me all
the stories, really interesting, the way she tells us. She tells us when English
people live in India, then when India had been free how the people kill
each other.' She pauses, then adds, 'I think we all share our life with
each other.' Through these stories Gurdeep's mother and grandmother
bind their family together with inherited memories and a shared interpretation of history: Gurdeep listens and becomes part of this cultural
tradition.

Gurdeep's mother describes some of the kinship patterns within the
family structure:

> We are living with the family together, my husband's parents and his sister
> and our three children. We live together and we help each other, so we teach
> our children to help each other and do all sorts of things for everybody. We
> teach them from the beginning because we always live together and we're
> expecting the same thing from them when we get older and they have to live
> with us and look after us.

In this way Gurdeep hears the story of his own life unfolding. As the
eldest son he will one day have to shoulder the heavy responsibilities his
father now carries. He has already begun to understand, too, that he has
a personal history, unique to him. Part of his life is recorded in his
photograph album, which he looks at every day, seeing himself first as

a young baby, then as a toddler, and now as a four-year-old. Each photograph tells its own story, and Gurdeep weaves each of these, with enormous economy, into a single narrative:

> When I was in hospital I was a baby ... there's my mum holding me ... I had a needle in my arm and then I went out ... I'm coming out of hospital ... now I'm going home ... this is my grandma and mum and my auntie holding me ... I'm grown up now.

Leafing through his album Gurdeep reconstructs some of the key events in his life as they have been told to him, and in so doing learns to make sense of the passing of time from babyhood onwards. He gives himself a history by constantly repeating and memorising, searching out what the past has to offer him and making connections. Gurdeep celebrates and enjoys his life all over again, every day, giving it renewed meaning and taking sustenance from the telling. His album helps him to make a narrative of his first four years: the frame around each photograph, the beginning and end of the album, act as boundaries to his life. The empty pages stretch ahead. At the moment the cultural and religious expectations of his family and community are in sharp focus; the culture of Western society, which he meets on television or when he's out shopping or playing with his toys, will be increasingly in the foreground now he is at school.

Around him at home there are novels written in English, magazines, English and Punjabi newspapers, shopping catalogues and calendars. Gurdeep reads advertisements on television, the writing on cereal boxes, mugs, and the information sheet that tells him the names of the Transformers. According to his mother he is usually the first to pick up birthday cards, wedding invitations and letters that arrive, and these are read to him as they are passed around for everyone to see. He shuffles through his mother's domestic papers when she opens her file and he is interested in the writing and patterns on coins and notes. He sees his parents writing in Punjabi and English and tries to copy them. In the temple there are notices around in Punjabi and English saying 'Silence please', 'Ladies' Shoes' and 'Men's Shoes'.

The family borrow books from the library every month and Gurdeep's mother reads detective novels, and gardening and cookery books, all written in English. They always borrow one book from the library especially for Gurdeep; 'It pleases him, just getting books,' his parents explain, adding: 'he gives the book to us when he wants to listen to the story.'

Both parents are concerned that he should not choose a book that is too difficult for him. They have a clear view of the reading process as they see it: 'We just look at the book. If it's a hard one, then we tell him that you can't read this and you are too young, then we find another book with a few words, few sentences or more pictures.'

The Guru Granth Saheb, the sacred Sikh text, is about five times the length of the Bible, and it is the visual and spiritual focus at the temple where Gurdeep's family worship each Sunday, sitting cross-legged, heads covered and feet bare, his father on one side of the room and his mother, aunt and the children on the other, facing towards the holy book; sometimes they talk, or greet other families, and sometimes Gurdeep's mother joins in the singing and prayers. The Guru Granth Saheb lies under a carved wooden canopy and behind the book, facing everybody, the priest sits cross-legged and mediates the holy words to his audience. At night the book is taken to a rest room where it lies in a special bed until three o'clock the following morning, when it is carefully replaced on the altar. Gurdeep's family hold in their possession a copy of the Guru Granth Saheb, bound in two separate parts.

One day Gurdeep's mother showed me all the family's holy books. Before she opened the cabinet where they are kept we washed our hands and Gurdeep's sister chose to cover her head and wash her mouth. Gurdeep's mother reached to the back of the shelves and carefully drew out prayer books and stories of the lives of the Gurus, each covered with gold and purple cloth. Then she showed me a volume of the Guru Granth Saheb and unwrapped the fold of cloth to reveal a large and beautifully bound book. The family read and study the text:

> Sometimes my mother-in-law reads aloud and we all sit and sometimes I read and they all listen, but sometimes we call other people and have a bit of sermoning. It's like having a small function. We invite people and we borrow a holy book from the temple and the lady sings and we read the hymns together or say the prayers and the music is played by some ladies and then we have a meal afterwards.

At other times Gurdeep sits cross-legged with his mother on the settee while she reads to him from the holy book. 'Gurdeep sits with me and he wants to touch it,' his mother explains. 'I tell him the words are in Punjabi.' The holy book emphasises a life of service and good living, and responsibility to the family and the community. Gurdeep will come to understand that he has a duty to do useful work, to raise a family, and to take an active part in society; that he should eat a healthy diet, keep himself clean and dress correctly. Gurdeep brings with him to school, in his neat dress, his self-discipline and his honesty, some of the high values which his culture and religion expect of him.

In this way the Guru Granth Saheb serves as a continuing spiritual teacher and guide for Gurdeep's family and community. It gives Gurdeep a way of seeing his community in control of cultural and literacy practices, thus providing a framework for keeping in touch not only with Sikh culture but with the distant homelands of his parents and grandparents: a kind of portable homeland for the Sikh population in Coventry.

In Gurdeep's home, telling or reading stories from India is an important way for the family to maintain their cultural identity and their history. His mother remembers:

> In India when it's really hot weather and we sleep outside, we take the beds out and make them very close to each other. We sit on the beds and Grandfather and Grandmother used to tell stories. We look at the stars and the birds flying in the evening, then the old person would tell the stories. It's very common in India.

In remembering, her reminiscence is itself a story. Now, when she has time and isn't tired, she tells stories to Gurdeep in Punjabi. Her stories serve to remind me that he is the inheritor of a rich oral tradition of storytelling. 'Telling by yourself makes them a bit different,' she says, 'you can add a few things more when you are telling by yourself.' In the telling, she maintains the continuity of traditional values which come directly from the oral tradition, and her fables thus remind Gurdeep that there is a right way for him to live his life. Here, then, is one of her moral tales:

> Once upon a time in a village there was a pond. There lived so many fishes and a tortoise, it's quite a big one. They are all very friendly and there's every day two birds come to eat the fishes. They stand near the pond and talk to the tortoise. They became very friendly.
>
> One year there was no rain. The pond was getting dry and day by day all the fishes were dying without water and one day both birds were talking and the tortoise heard them saying that there's going to be no rain and the pond is getting dry and we can't get food here, so we're going to move somewhere else to another pond.
>
> When the tortoise heard the friends talking like that he was worried also where he's going to because he can't fly, he can't walk very fast. So he begged

the birds to take him away with them because as they were friends. The birds they listen to the tortoise and they start to think how to take him to another city, or to another country, to another pond. Then after quite a lot of thinking they decide they'll have a big stick. They both would hold the big stick in their mouths and the tortoise have to hold the big stick in the middle so he can fly.

Once they decide, they found a big stick. Both birds were flying with the big stick and the tortoise was holding the middle. And the birds told the tortoise as he was a chatterbox, 'When we are flying with you please don't talk.'

'I won't talk.' Then they start their journey. They're flying. And when they were flying, they were flying over a village and there were some children. They were playing in the field and one child he saw the birds flying and he told the others, 'Look, the tortoise fly!' and all the children started to laugh at the tortoise and they all started to make noise. 'Oh look, the tortoise is flying!'

When the tortoise heard that he couldn't stop to say anything. He talk. He tried to say something. He opened his mouth and he fall. He fall hard on the floor and he died.

From this story we have to learn the lesson that don't try to be a fool when somebody tries to tease you. Think what you have to say. Think about yourself first, then answer back.

I know of no stories in school that Gurdeep has heard which follow the form of the moral tale as closely as this. In fact, the culture of the school presents Gurdeep with a different form of narrative; the fairy tales he enjoys come from a European tradition (*Teeny Tiny and the Witch Woman* is his current favourite) and though these tales contain their own ethical code, and the central character often learns valuable lessons about the right way to live, the formula is different: in the end good triumphs and evil is punished. I can only guess at how far these two cultural perspectives on narrative have influenced his own stories, but certainly the Transformer story he told after two terms in school catches the form of the fairy tale where good triumphs and evil gets its just deserts:

All the baddy evils came to fight and Optimus Prime quickly changed. Then he got his gun. Then he quickly fighted. Then the fight was finished and the baddy ones were all burned ... and Optimus Prime won again.

Towards the end of his first year in school Gurdeep wanted to hear *Goldilocks and the Three Bears* over and over again. He told me that it was now his favourite story. Here, he reads part of the story with his teacher:

TEACHER: 'So Goldilocks climbed up on to the very big bed but it was too ...'
GURDEEP: Lumpy.
TEACHER: 'Too lumpy. Then she climbed on to the medium-sized bed but it was too ...'
GURDEEP: Smooth.
TEACHER: Yes. 'Then Goldilocks lay down on the tiny little bed. It was just ...'
GURDEEP: Right.·
TEACHER: 'And soon she was fast asleep.' There she is lying on the bed.

Gurdeep's teacher lends him the support of a skilled language user while he grows towards an understanding of the text. In time, as he achieves independence, he will incorporate her role into his own reading. Similarly, when Gurdeep and I share *Where The Wild Things Are* I pause in the narrative to ask him for information that I feel will give him a deeper understanding of Max's motives and fears:

HM: '... and he sailed off through night and day and in and out of weeks and almost over a year to where the wild things are.' Who is he sailing away from?
GURDEEP: From his mother.
HM: Why?
GURDEEP: 'Cos he's very naughty boy.
HM: Why does he want to go away?
GURDEEP: 'Cos he doesn't like her.

At school when Gurdeep reads with an adult, the story-reading sessions nearly always take the form of a dialogue, but at home story time takes place within different social and cultural traditions. At night Gurdeep and his sister share the same story, usually read by their father before they go to sleep in their bunk beds. He reads them a book chosen from the library, either written in English or with a dual English and Punjabi text, and chosen to reflect the culture of India 'so that they know their own culture, the background', he explains. 'I stop and ask if there's a hard word I think they might not have understood,' he goes on to say.

One of the Indian folk tales he reads is called, significantly, *The Naughty Mouse*, the title giving a clear moral lead on how the story is to be read and interpreted. Gurdeep's father introduces the book and begins reading. After the first sentence he pauses to ask if they understand.

FATHER: The title of the story is 'The Naughty Mouse'. Right. Listen, children. 'There was once a very naughty and cunning mouse. He was always looking for mischief.' Do you both understand?

They say they do and he continues reading for about three minutes. Halfway through the story he pauses to see if Gurdeep has understood and to share his own observations about the mouse's character:

FATHER: Cheeky mouse, ain't he?
GURDEEP: Yes, he's a naughty mouse.
FATHER: He's a naughty mouse.
GURDEEP: 'Cos he's ... he's a naughty mouse. He hits everyone, doesn't he? Therefore he's naughty.

Then he reads to the end of the story. When they reach the end Gurdeep pleads for another story – 'Read this one now! Read this one!' and his father begins *Nanda in India*, the story of a boy living in England who goes to India to visit his grandmother. Gurdeep hums to himself as he listens to his father read and he and his sister appear to adopt a listening role. But halfway through the book, when Gurdeep's father has been reading for a few minutes, he comes to a place in the story where Nanda is taken to the market to see the snake charmers. As he turns the page, Gurdeep suddenly interrupts:

GURDEEP: I want to see the snake again.
FATHER: Pardon?
GURDEEP: I want to see the snake again.
FATHER: You want to see the snake again?
GURDEEP: Yeah.
FATHER: There it is.
GURDEEP: I went to see it in the cage, in the cage.
FATHER: Where?
GURDEEP: In the cage. Look!
SISTER: Where? Twycross zoo?
GURDEEP: Yeah. They have to put them ... put it in the box and you have to get a snake, you don't have to hold it, you have to put it in a small box and put it in paper and close it and put water in there and it can swim.
FATHER: I don't know what you're talking about. OK. Sit down.
GURDEEP: A snake!
FATHER: Listen, OK.

Gurdeep's detailed account of something he has seen, perhaps at the zoo or perhaps on television, can't be framed and extended by his father because the two don't share the same background general knowledge and perhaps also because father and son don't share the same sociocultural knowledge of reading and listening patterns. Although Gurdeep's father is patient and polite, he seems uncomfortable when Gurdeep takes control by moving too far from the text and initiating more of a conversation than his father can handle. If this is so, then there is no way of building a context for Gurdeep's snake story to develop, even with his sister's help. Gurdeep's father could have responded by telling his own real life story about snake charmers in India, but clearly this could not have felt appropriate for him. There is nothing for it but to continue reading on to the next page, which describes the procession through the Indian village. Gurdeep interjects again when he sees an elephant in the illustration:

GURDEEP: An elephant and a zoo.
FATHER: It's not a zoo. It's some sort of procession.

Then, perhaps sensing Gurdeep's interest, he adds:

FATHER: It's a huge elephant, isn't it?
GURDEEP: Yes.
FATHER: Very well decorated. Mmm ... Must carry on.

But Gurdeep wishes to talk about the elephant:

GURDEEP: I want an elephant at home that can sit on here and can walk. They don't run. They just walk like this ...
SISTER: Slowly.
FATHER: Mmm. OK.

Once again Gurdeep's father is compelled to return to the text. Why does he feel the need to do this? Possibly he is tired after a day at work; perhaps, too, the effort of sustaining a conversation in English – the second language of all three participants – is too much. And I think there may be another reason which lies within the father's own ways of listening to and making sense of texts. He is used to taking the role of listener himself at the temple when the words of the sacred book are mediated to him through the priest without interruption. He associates the modes of reader and listener, in other words, with the ritual relationship of reader authoritatively mediating texts and listener receiving, actively but without interrupting, and it may seem appropriate for his children to do this when he reads to them. So although his responses may appear repressive to some infant teachers, they are in fact a gift of cultural inheritance to Gurdeep and his sister.

And perhaps Gurdeep is modelling himself on his father when he retells *Where the Wild Things Are* to his classmate Simon. He is interested in sharing the enjoyment of the story with Simon, but clearly wants to hold on to the telling:

SIMON: Read the book!
GURDEEP: I can read it.
SIMON: Go on then.
GURDEEP: His mother said one day he has been naughty, putting his ... he was he was hammering, putting the golden ...

The reading is suspended for a time while the children play with the Wild Thing puppets, then Gurdeep begins an exuberant performance of retelling:

> Then he's going to kill the dog. Dog ... ranned ... he runned away. He went to sleep with no dinner. The bedroom grow ... grewed and and grewed. It became ... mother said no ... ah ... no I missed the other page [turns back]. Ah he said mother I'll eat you up. The ... the ... garden growed and grewed and growed the ... his mother said Your ... I called you wild Max. He buyed ... he buyed a new boat he have to sail right to monsters. The ... he he he went in the private boat that came out of ... Out of the water came a big monster and he [blows] did that and Max was scared then they went down. Down he went. He said I'm coming out. They gnashed their terrible ... gnashed they gnashed their terrible ... ter ... eyes. Tashed their terrible. Tashed their terrible teeth and tashed terr – showed their terrible claws. Then Max said Don't just get off this ground. I'm going to be the king. He danced and he danced ... and danced and had a fight. Then he said goodbye and they said we'll eat you up. They gnashed their terrible ...

As Gurdeep remakes this story for himself, I recall his mother's thoughts on the storytelling process: 'Telling by yourself makes them a bit different. You can add a few things when you are telling by yourself.' Now Gurdeep uses his own developing skills as a storyteller, and as a reader, to retell this story for himself and Simon. As he reconstructs this story we see him doing several important things. First, he is learning to control the pace of his own reading – it is his choice whether he speeds up, or slows down, pauses or repeats parts of the story; in other words, he is learning to become autonomous in his reading. Secondly, he uses some of the formal language of the story – 'private boat', 'It became' – and incorporates this into his own retelling, even though he sometimes gets it slightly mixed-up: 'They gnashed their terrible ... gnashed they gnashed their terrible, ter ... eyes. Tashed their terrible. Tashed their terrible teeth and ...' This attempt to recall the tone and rhythm of written language represents the beginnings of a mastery of a new genre. Thirdly, Gurdeep is beginning to learn the conventions of book-reading. He knows how to hold a book, where to open it, that he should look from left to right along the page, and when to turn over. Fourthly, he also knows that there is a relationship between story and reality and he can take himself in and out of the story as he wishes: '... mother said no ... ah ... no I missed the other page [turns back]. Ah he said mother ...'

I have several vivid images of Gurdeep as a reader: sitting cross-legged on his settee at home and leaning against his mother while she reads to him from the holy book; sitting on the carpet at the temple while he hears the Guru Granth Saheb being read to his family and community; sitting on the carpet at school with the rest of his class listening to *Goldilocks and the Three Bears*; sitting beside his teacher on the settee in his classroom while she shares a book with him. Being a reader in Gurdeep's terms means being open to all these experiences, and more too, learning what to value and what to discard, so that he feels part of each reading community he enters. Perhaps more than anyone else, he has begun to teach me what learning to read is all about.

2

Gemma[1]

Gemma looked serious as she came into school with her mother, and as they went past the nursery room where Gemma had spent the previous year her mother said she felt Gemma's hand holding hers more tightly. She wasn't surprised to find that Gemma was nervous this morning; it had taken her a few weeks to settle into the nursery a year ago. Gemma cried as her teacher welcomed her, and the mother judged that she ought to go away quietly, since the parting was clearly going to be difficult. She said goodbye to her tearful daughter, promising to collect her at the end of the school day, and guiltily made her way home.

Despite her tears, Gemma's mother feels that her daughter, at four years and four months, is more advanced than she was at that age, and is convinced that Gemma's nursery experience has made a difference to her development. She regrets leaving school herself without a good education and wants her three children to do better than she did. 'I'd like Gemma to get something,' she says, 'not just go into a factory like I did.'

Gemma lives with her family in a three-bedroomed council house a couple of blocks from school. The houses are pre-war and were built to provide homes for the growing number of skilled workers employed in the north-east of the city in the late 1930s. Now, the houses are being modernised by the council and Gemma's parents welcome this. At the end of the terraced block a Hindu temple is nearing completion and some white residents worry about the changes this might mean for their community. I learn about this as we sit in the front room, drinking tea. Gemma and her younger sister, Jade, sit on their father's knee and he holds them tenderly. The gas fire is on, and it's warm and comfortable. The television is on quietly, and Gemma and Jade are watching a cartoon. Jamie, their older brother, is out playing. The dog, Sandy, is barking in the kitchen. She had pups not long ago. There is a music centre in the alcove and ornaments on the shelves above. Some of Jamie's school books lie on the carpet.

I don't see any other books around and Gemma's mother tells me that she has little time to read, though at one time she used to read *Mills & Boon* books for entertainment. Now, though, with three children to look after, domestic chores take priority. When she was younger she belonged to the library, but she hasn't borrowed books for a long time. She says it's too risky bringing them home; she is afraid that Jade will damage them. She writes an occasional note, perhaps to a friend or relative, 'saying I'm going to see you on Thursday or something like that', but she prefers talking to people rather than writing to them. Gemma's father, a welder by trade, was made redundant from the Talbot car plant three years ago, and now has time on his hands. He reads the *Star* or the *Coventry Evening Telegraph* in detail, most days.

I ask about Gemma's interest in books and her parents tell me they haven't noticed her taking any real interest, though she will occasionally look at Jamie's school books. They have an early memory of her owning some thick cardboard books when she was small and they remember teaching her to say the words 'cats' and 'mice' from one of the books. But they were afraid to give her more books in case she ripped them, or scribbled in them. Gemma has never been told a bedtime story: she and her younger sister go to bed at six-thirty each night, and fall straight to sleep. At nursery Gemma used to sit and listen quietly and unresponsively to stories being read to her and her real interest, her teacher said, seemed to be in painting or crayoning.

But even though Gemma's parents are not book readers or book collectors there is nevertheless a respect for literacy in the home and an expectation that Gemma will begin to take an interest in reading when she starts school, and that this interest will be fostered at home; indeed, her mother tells me: 'We'll have to get some more decent books. I'll be reading with her now she's starting school. Now she's old enough to appreciate it.'

One sunny morning in early July, a few weeks before she is to start school, I visit Gemma again in her home and ask her to draw a picture. She is now four years and two months old, and we sit at the kitchen table while her mother talks to a friend in the front room. Jamie sits with

us and watches with interest while she draws. (Figure 1). 'That's a milk
bottle with a lady in it,' she tells us. I ask her to write 'milk bottle' and
she does so, saying, 'That says "milk bottle",' and then she writes, saw-
tooth fashion, representations of people she knows, each time saying as
she writes, 'That says ...' together with the name of the person or animal
she represents.

Figure 1

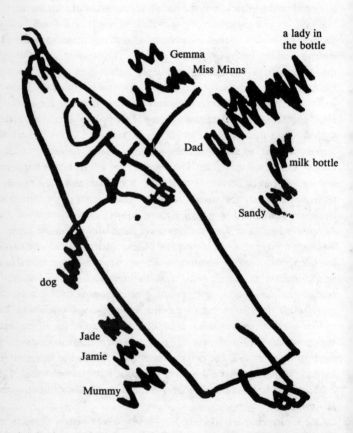

a lady in
the bottle

Gemma
Miss Minns

Dad

milk bottle

Sandy

dog

Jade
Jamie

Mummy

There is no doubt that Gemma has developed an interest in the uses
of print and has discovered for herself the symbolic function of writing.
She has learned that writing is different from drawing, and carries a

meaning of its own. She also knows that writing moves from left to right across the page (at no time did she try to write in the opposite direction). At this point in her development she is not able to make a unique sign for each name, and the meaning of each ⋁⋀⋁ is dependent on the context of her picture and the people she knows. The number of zigzags she produces for each name varies according to her perception of the respective sizes of the people represented (see, for instance, 'Dad' and 'Gemma').

Where did she begin to learn what writing is? Her mother has certainly noticed that she is beginning to pay attention to print in a way she has never done before. I can identify six specific occasions – two from her time in the nursery, the rest from home – that underlie her growing understanding of the processes of reading and writing. In the nursery she used to watch her teacher handle story books and listened to stories read to her daily in the year before she came to school; she also watched as her teacher wrote her name on each drawing, painting or card she made before taking it home.

At home Gemma's mother has noticed her watching her father do the crossword in the newspaper. One day she took her own pencil and paper and announced that she was going to do a crossword too. In the supermarket she has begun to pay attention to the food her parents buy, noticing the difference between peas and beans, 'though I think she goes by the colour of the can', says her mother. And she may be right. One day, a few weeks before starting school, Gemma was looking through a drawer and found the birthday cards she had had for her fourth birthday, three months before. 'Is that my name?' she asked her mother, pointing to the printed verse on one of the cards. 'No, that's not your name. That's your name there,' her mother explained, pointing it out to her. And a week or so later, after drawing a picture, she asked, 'Mum, will you help me do my name?' Her mother held her own hand over Gemma's and guided her hand as she wrote. It was at this time, too, that Gemma began to show an interest in Jamie's school books.

If I had never observed Gemma at home and talked to her parents, I might never have known about her awakening interest in literacy before she started school. Indeed, I might have concluded that since she did not appear to be much interested in stories, did not have books of her own and did not visit the library with her family, she might be slower to learn to read and write than children from homes where literacy was more in evidence. Certainly, the kinds of formal language she will meet in story books at school may appear strange to her.

Today, her first at school, Gemma listens with the other children while their teacher reads a story; and she listens again when her teacher explains that she can choose a book to take home to read. She looks through the books on the shelves and in the library outside the classroom and chooses *I'll Teach My Dog 100 Words*. This is her first experience of choosing a book to read. At home time, when her mother met her, Gemma took the book out of her bag, showed it to her mother, and asked her to read it. That significant act of choosing a book, and asking her mother to read it to her, signalled an important development in the relationship between mother and daughter: in partnership with a book. The teacher's invitation to take books home to read and share has made the act of reading a socially significant practice for Gemma and her mother. Gemma is, in fact, bringing the act of sharing and enjoying a book back into the household. Her mother observed later: 'Now that she's bringing books home from school she can't wait to bring them in and open them and I say to her, "After tea!" but she wants it there and then. "Read it to me now!" she says.'

It is not easy for Gemma's mother to make this time available, and since Gemma and her sister are both in bed by six-thirty, the organisation of time becomes a crucial factor in preparing the evening meal, washing up and getting the girls ready for bed, and I understand why Gemma's mother says she didn't 'really have time for reading with Gemma' before she came to school. Now, though, she plans the reading time: 'If it's chips for tea, I can sit down, but if I'm doing a dinner I say we'll do it after dinner.'

There isn't time every evening, certainly, and there is no doubt that it's easier to make a space for reading at the weekend, but Gemma and her mother read with enough frequency for her to observe Gemma's progress: 'She brought a book home with animals in it and she knew every one,' she observes. When they are reading together they both focus on the story rather than the meaning of individual words or letters, and they play together at reading in the same way they might play with a jigsaw, or dress a doll. There is pleasure in the joint effort, as they enter imaginatively into the world of the book. Mother and daughter use a different kind of talk together: for the first time Gemma's mother reads the words of a text aloud and Gemma listens to the texture of written language.

Six weeks after starting school, Gemma and her mother read *Me In Puddles* together. Jade listened too, and so three members of the family were sharing this book together; an event that would have been difficult to imagine before Gemma started school. Gemma's mother begins by reading the title of the book, then she reads several pages before pausing and setting up a dialogue for Gemma to respond to:

MOTHER: 'I make puddles on the floor. There are clean puddles and dirty puddles. I take water from the dirty puddles and put it in the clean puddles. Now I have two dirty puddles.' Uggh! Isn't it dirty?
GEMMA: Uggh! ...

Gemma expresses distaste and her mother continues reading, but Gemma interjects in order to establish the meaning of the text for herself by commenting on the illustration and trying out her own reading of the text; her 'that says ...' reminds me powerfully of the way she interpreted her own symbolic saw-tooth marks around her milk bottle drawing (see Figure 1). That same intellectual process of making language mean is at work here:

MOTHER: 'The raindrops make lots of little – '
GEMMA: And the man and that says I am under an umbrella. When the rain stops the umbrella goes on that man.

It is as if Gemma's mother knows instinctively that her daughter needs to make sense of the text in this way. She stops reading as soon as Gemma interjects and then responds to her daughter's comment by building on it with an explanation:

MOTHER: Yeah, that's right. Covers him 'cos of the rain.
GEMMA: Like you, Mum.
MOTHER: Yeah.

Gemma and her mother use conversational talk to construct the meaning together and to establish the connection between Gemma's first-hand experience and the text. Gemma recalls seeing her mother with an umbrella as she looks at the illustration – 'like you, Mum' – and thus relates this part of the story to an experience in her own life. Her mother's encouragement shows her that it is a worthwhile thing to do.

When Gemma feels she can read a page back to her mother, she allows
this, and Gemma uses her memory of what has just been read to
interpret the illustration and construct this reading:

MOTHER: 'The wind makes ripples on the puddles. I like the splishy splashy
   sound the water makes, when I'm splashing in the puddles.'
GEMMA: I'm splashing in the puddles. I'm walking in the puddles. Splish. Splash.
   That says splish splash. That says I'm walking in the puddles. That says I got
   my my my boats in the puddles.

When they reach the end of the book Gemma's mother asks Gemma
to read the story back to her. As Gemma does so, her mother will take
responsibility for her daughter's learning by accepting her version of the
story, and responding positively to the meaning Gemma makes. She will
make no attempt to make Gemma read the actual words of the text, so
there is never any sense that Gemma will not succeed. This is of central
importance to Gemma's whole approach to herself as a learner. Her
mother sets her daughter up to behave as a reader, with herself and her
younger sister as audience. She allows Gemma to find her own way into
the text:

GEMMA: That's me in the puddle. I got dirt all over me. When my mummy
   don't see me I got dirty and all wet. [Actual text: 'Sometimes I creep into
   a puddle when mummy is very busy and not looking at me.']

Gemma's interpretation shows that she has been attending closely to the
meaning. She hesitates before the next page and her mother helps her
by asking, 'What's he doing there?'

GEMMA: I can see myself in the puddle. [Actual text: 'Down in the clean puddles
   I can see someone who looks like me.']

Gemma gets inside the narrative now; she becomes the 'I' of the story
as she fictionalises herself by moving into the text, and when she reads,
'I am splashing in the water and walking in the muddy puddles', she is
more than likely making reference to something she does, or would like
to do, herself. Gemma's sentence is also extremely literary: 'I can see
myself in the puddle' is the language of the book. Her normal everyday
conversation does not show this formal patterning. As she listens to the
'voice' on the page she begins to talk like the book, taking the structures
of the written text and incorporating them into her own reading. This
makes her reading powerful; she is learning to have a new control over

language as she echoes the formal language she has heard her mother read in the story. And there is a feeling of achievement and contentment as the retelling reaches its conclusion:

MOTHER: You like to move in the muddy puddles, don't you?
GEMMA: Yes. No and I likes I likes I fallen down in the puddles.
MOTHER: Yes.
GEMMA: And get all dirty and all wet. So I'm going to bed now. I'll go out tomorrow.
MOTHER: And play in the puddles.
GEMMA: And play in the puddles.
MOTHER: And get all wet.

Gemma's mother cannot remember how she learned to read herself as a child, and she has no memories of being read to. Neither of her parents read books, though her father read the newspaper. Yet helping Gemma to learn to read in this way seems as natural to her as helping her to learn to walk or talk. 'I used to read books at one time,' she explains, 'so it just comes naturally.' But there is more to it than this. She is able to respond to what Gemma is doing with a book in much the same supportive way as a teacher would (though she decries her own flat tones as she reads aloud to Gemma, and wishes she could read as well as Gemma's teacher). She observes sensitively what happens as she and Gemma read together:

> When you're reading her stories she takes it all in. 'Cos if I read the book over again to her she's telling me what's coming on the page. On one book she says, 'and he told her off' and before I turn the page over she knew it was on the next page.

There are echoes here of her early memories and observations of Gemma learning to walk:

> I used to sit at one end and her dad used to sit a bit nearer and I used to say, 'Come on', and we used to do it for hours. She wasn't long walking.

And talk:

> We'd say everything we'd seen, like. I think 'dog' was quite a quick word with her because she liked dogs. Then 'nan' and 'grandad'. She seemed to pick them up. She more or less learned herself.

Gemma learned to walk and talk within her family; now, at school, her whole society has widened and she is part of a new social group, subject to new conventions, new ways of using language. She spends time watching in quiet concentration as other children read, do jigsaws or draw, and she joins in when she wants to. Sometimes she chooses not to, and sits on the settee, self-possessed, with her teddy. She is surrounded by print, much more than she has seen around her at home – picture books, picture-story books, labels, notices, lists and folders, and she sees around her children reading for themselves in different ways: sharing a book together on the carpet or settee, browsing through a book box on their own, listening to a taped story, reading a book into the tape-recorder with the microphone attached so they can hear their own voices echoed back to them, reading a book to the whole class, reading with the teacher, education assistant, or with older children who come into the classroom. Sometimes Gemma chooses to share a book with a friend, and because she has no fear of failure, and trusts herself to learn with help from a teacher – whether that teacher is her mother, her teacher at school, or another child in the class – she asks for assistance when she needs it. Here, she shares *Goldilocks and the Three Bears* with Geeta, who is the same age, and recalls the beginning of the story in her own words as she turns the pages:

GEMMA: Porridge was too hot and they set off out in the woods. Long time ago. Her name was Goldilocks. Don't know this bit.

'Don't know this bit' means, I think, that she has forgotten what comes next in the narrative, not that she feels she can't read the text. She's trying to recall a story she has heard before, and her memory has been jogged by a picture of the bears leaving the house, and the porridge on the table. Her 'long time ago' is significant, for it echoes the language of the tale. Geeta takes over now, and goes back to the beginning as she supports Gemma in telling the story:

GEETA: Once upon a time there was Goldilocks. She came in and she and she's nearly open the door and nobody was there. I got that book.

Geeta does not move the narrative forward, but she does focus it in a slightly different way, concentrating on Goldilocks entering the house. Gemma now has the confidence to continue:

GEMMA: Too sweet said Goldilocks. Daddy bear ... too hot. Tries mummy bear. Too lumpy. Tries mummy bear ... tries baby bear ... the best, so baby bear now just right. So she ate it all up. Don't know it.

She has remembered the formula for the story, shaped by its pattern of repetition, and now needs support again in the telling. Once more Geeta helps:

GEETA: She she sitting in baby chair and she crashed. Really sorry. She sitting ...

Gemma's memory is jogged again:

GEMMA: I know it. She went upstairs and she tries daddy's bed. Too high. Tried mummy's bed. Too high. Tried mummy's bed. Too ...
GEETA: Lumpy.
GEMMA: Lumpy. Tries baby bear's bed. Just right.

This time it is Gemma who remembers what comes next. She takes over the telling as she recalls what happened as Goldilocks went upstairs, and Geeta becomes the listener. Gemma seems to know that 'high' will not do for the description of mummy bear's bed and seems to struggle to find the right word. Geeta tells her; it's 'lumpy' and Gemma accepts her correction. So it is that these two young girls make learning happen for each other as they construct the story together, learning how to learn from each other in a context made possible for them by their teacher.

When Gemma had been in school for ten weeks, she took another important step in her development as a reader and writer. Supported by her teacher, she became the author of a book (Figure 2). Gemma listened as her teacher read *Burglar Bill* and then drew a burglar. Sensing her interest, her teacher asked her if she wanted to make her own Burglar Bill book. She said she did, and her teacher made her a small book. Gemma dictated, and her teacher wrote:

> The big burglar
> The little burglar
> The little burglar stole a pencil
> The big burglar stole a rubber
> The policeman hurt the burglars

Figure 2: Gemma dictated and her teacher wrote ...

Gemma illustrated the book, then read it to her teacher and to me. The significance of this event is twofold: first, there is a sense of celebration. When her teacher put the finished book in her hand it was a way of reflecting Gemma's success as a writer back to her. Now, the story is hers to read and to share. Secondly, and more generally, she is being encouraged by a sensitive teacher to learn and discover how to read and write in the same supportive way her parents helped her to walk and talk: with the expectation of success.

Some time after this she showed me a book she made for Jade. It was called *The Burglars* (Figure 3). As she showed me the illustrations she told me the story:

The big burglar puts the things in a bag

The big burglar took the clothes
The policeman got the burglars
The big burglar was sad

The writing on the first page, ммо , stands for 'the burglars' and clearly shows the two 'm's from Gemma's name. I recall that Gemma was already differentiating between drawing and writing before she came to school. Now she is beginning to pay attention to the characters that make up conventional writing, using those predominantly in her own name, to say precisely what she wants them to say in the context of the illustration and at a fixed moment in time.

Book-making continues to be important for Gemma and in March, her seventh month in school, this activity was extended by Serena, a nine-year-old in one of the Upper School classes who came to work with a younger child. She wrote quickly, as Gemma dictated this book to her (Figure 4):

This is my mum
I like my mum
My mum has yellow hair
My mum likes me
My mum takes me to the park
My mummy pushes me on the swing
My mum can wash the pots

Then Gemma illustrated her book. It has the quality of a book written and produced at high speed, in response to a great need on the part of Gemma. Serena said afterwards, 'Gemma put all the ideas into it. It was nothing really from me. She likes her family. She thinks about them all the time. She puts them in her stories.'

With this model book in her head, Gemma produced a book by herself for Jade and her mother to read (Figure 5). It has five pages and Gemma read her own writing back to me, using five of the sentences about her mother that she had dictated to Serena. Her writing seems to be made up of an upper-case E, O, G, and possibly D, an upper- and lower-case I, an upper- and lower-case A, a lower-case m, a number 5, and three more characters that may be her first attempts at forming other characters. Although she knows so few characters, she has been able to vary their use to make five sentences.

Gemma arrived at school with an emergent literacy of her own and

Figure 3: A burglar book for Jade

The Burglars

The burglar puts the things in a bag.

The big burglar took the clothes.

The policeman got the burglars

The big burglar was sad.

Figure 4: Part of the story Serena wrote and Gemma dictated ...

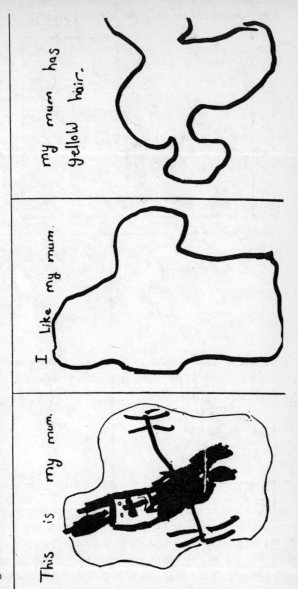

This is my mum.

I Like my mum.

my mum has yellow hair.

Figure 5: Part of the book for Jade and Mum

This is my mum.

I like my mum.

My mum has yellow hair.

in the classroom context has been able to develop this, taking for herself the identity of reader and writer. Part of Gemma's early success can be attributed to the way her teacher has set up a comfortable context in the classroom where she feels at ease and can learn to read and write at her own pace, building on the skills she already had when she arrived at school. Gemma's delight in language is possible because her teacher and her mother concentrate on her enjoyment of stories: they key into her developing awareness of language but put no pressure on her to learn any mechanical skills at the expense of meaning or enjoyment. She is free, then, to learn other things to do with reading: about the formal literary language of well-written story books, and the excitement of authoring books of her own. But perhaps above all she is learning about her own relationship with books and with herself as a reader, appearing poised and confident as she enters into a very special learning partnership with those around her.

3

Anthony

The people in Anthony's household, his mother and older sister Paulette, both read and write for their own purposes and pleasure, so it isn't really surprising that Anthony shares their delight in stories and wants to gain a mastery over reading and writing for himself. And since his mother and Paulette have both set themselves up to be his teachers, there is a good chance that Anthony's interest in literacy will be carried back and forth between home and school.

Anthony came along to his classroom quite confidently on his first day at school. His mother, a nursing auxiliary, had arranged to be on leave so she could bring him and see he settled down happily. She had no real fears that he would find his first day at school unsettling as he'd already had the experience of attending two nurseries and a play group, and of being cared for by a childminder while she worked, so he was used to being with different adults and children and learning to play in new surroundings. Paulette had also told him that she had begun her school life in this same room four years before, and this perhaps gave him some feeling of security.

Anthony's classroom is the largest in the corridor, and when the school was built in the 1950s it was specially designed for young children. As Anthony and his mother look round they can see a large half-timbered playhouse, a carpeted area where the children can read, or play with the bricks or train set, and share news and listen to stories; rows of shelves containing games, jigsaws and Lego sets, and a trolley for brushes and paints, glue and paste. There are red plastic boxes on every table, each with books in for the children to read, and there are more books on the shelves near the carpet. Anthony and his mother looked at the children's paintings and pictures that his teacher had already put on the wall and then, with a last reminder about eating all his dinner up, she left him playing contentedly with the toys.

The two children live with their mother in a terraced 1930s house near the school, in a quiet road where some of Anthony's classmates also live. We sit in comfortable chairs at one end of the through lounge and Paulette listens to our conversation and sometimes joins in. Anthony is watching television. There is a dining table at the far end of the room, where the family eat together at weekends, and leading off to the right is the kitchen. Anthony, Paulette and their mother form a close-knit family group: 'I'd like them to be around me all the time,' says their mother. She says they are company for her and for each other when she has to be away from them, and feels strongly that families belong together, especially since her own parents came to live in England and left her, angry and resentful, to be brought up by an auntie and grandfather in Barbados. Her time with her own two children is strictly rationed, however, since she has to work long hours, often leaving home at 6.30 a.m. and not returning until 8.30 p.m. in the evening. Her compensation for working this long shift is that she works just seven days each fortnight and the remainder of the time is her own, to be spent with the children and to organise her household.

Her own schooling in Barbados was much more formal than Anthony's will be, and she remembers being taught to read by learning 'the ABC from a blackboard'. She has memories, too, of her auntie and grandfather reading the Bible and of possessing a Bible of her own. Church on Sunday was obligatory and seemed to last 'nearly all day'. She recalls that 'everyone took a turn reading the Bible, including the children. Every child had a Bible and children were expected to learn verses by heart then stand at the altar and recite.'

Anthony's mother came to England when she was eleven and lived in London before coming to Coventry as a teenager. She remembers reading quite a lot when she lived in London, 'but now I don't read'. Recently a friend lent her Alice Walker's *The Color Purple*, but 'I just put the book down 'cos I couldn't get time to read it', she explains. She likes poetry and there is a framed poem on the wall, the words appearing below a photograph of two gulls flying off into the blue sky.

Sometimes Anthony's mother takes a book to work to read in her breaks, 'but you never seem to get time, so I just don't bother'. At home sometimes she reads the *Daily Mirror* and *Roots*, a black magazine that comes out monthly. Her cousin sends her the *Nation*, the newspaper from Barbados, and she enjoys reading that because 'I like to know what's going on at home'. On the living-room wall, above the gas fire, are two bright paintings of street scenes in Barbados, and she can recognise the shops portrayed and remember buying things from them. Paulette has visited the island with her godmother, but Anthony must wait until he is older.

The piece of writing that made most impression on Anthony's mother was a project she wrote on Barbados while she was at secondary school in Coventry. 'It's the whole story,' she says, 'from Christopher Columbus days,' and she's saving it for Paulette to read when she is older. Once she tried to write her own life story but became 'embarrassed' as she wrote and, perhaps to avoid facing difficult feelings, she 'stopped in the end'. She doesn't write much now, although sometimes she sits down and writes poems. 'I always have done,' she says. 'I get spates where I stop but I like writing. Like last night I tried to think of writing something; I couldn't so I packed it up. I've got to be in a good mood to sort of write.' She does write the occasional letter but says, 'I'm not a great writer of letters.' She writes shopping lists regularly.

Anthony's mother has identified her own needs as a reader and writer, even though these needs are frustrated by lack of time; she clearly knows the power of writing, and sees the value of literacy as a way of enhancing her own life. It is not surprising, therefore, that she is supportive of Anthony and Paulette as they learn to become readers and writers themselves.

Anthony has few books of his own and the family don't use the public library, but occasionally when time permits all three of them sit down and Anthony's mother reads one of Paulette's *Brer Rabbit* stories, one of a series kept safely in her wardrobe. Most of Anthony's books are the ones Paulette had when she was small. 'I don't see the point in buying another lot of books,' says his mother. 'He can use them.' Anthony has the taped story of *One Hundred and One Dalmatians* and his mother says he knows it well, though she feels he has 'just memorised it'. He likes nursery rhymes too, and the jingles from advertisements on television: 'When they come on he knows exactly what they're going to say,' his mother observes. He also appreciates jokes, too, and though he doesn't always get them right he demonstrates a growing awareness of control over language:

ANTHONY: Mum, do you want me to tell you a joke about the butter?
MUM: What is it?
ANTHONY: You can't spread it 'cos it might melt.

Anthony has his own bedroom, but never uses it. Instead he prefers to tuck himself into bed with Paulette, 'but everything is there ready for him when he's decided, "That is my room," ' says his mum. All his clothes are in his room, his wardrobe and his chest of drawers. At night, side by side in bed, it's Paulette who shares a bedtime story with him or reads him a version of *The Pied Piper* or *Tom Thumb*, or an alphabet book that belonged to her when she was his age. Sometimes Paulette reads his favourite story, one of his three versions of *Little Red Riding Hood*. At other times she takes a pencil and paper and shows him how to write.

Anthony's implicit knowledge of different uses of reading and writing is already there before he comes to school: he has seen story books and poetry read for pleasure and knows that books are to be valued and cared for, handed down and grown into like good clothes with plenty of wear left in them; and inside them are stories to enjoy and words to learn to read; he sees newspapers read and commented upon; he watches Paulette and his mother write for different purposes; he sees titles of his favourite television programmes, looks at advertisements on television, and reads food labels. The only time the three of them sit down as a family to watch television is when 'EastEnders' is on, but Anthony and Paulette watch Children's ITV every evening after school and Anthony particularly likes 'He-Man', 'She-Ra', 'Knight-Rider', 'Streethawk', 'The A-Team', 'Airwolf' and any cartoons. He can read cereal packets and recognises Cocopops and Weetabix as his two favourites. They normally go shopping together, and it's Anthony's job to put everything in the basket.

Paulette and her mother are nevertheless worried about Anthony's attitude to learning. 'I keep on telling him, "You've got to go to school in September", and he's still running about in the garden,' Paulette says despairingly. Her mother agrees. 'I hope he pulls himself together,' she says and adds, 'I think school will change him a lot.' She has given careful thought to the way she brings her children up and has clear views on how they learn. She recalls how Anthony learned to talk:

> I just let it come on its own 'cos it's better that way. They sort of pick up things here and there. If you push them too much it takes longer. They lose interest in what you're trying to tell them.

She has her own preferred way of sharing a book with Anthony and stresses how important it is to her that he shows he has understood the story. When they are together with a book she reads the story through to Anthony first of all 'so he gets the whole sort of picture of it' and then 'we go back through the book and I say to him, "What's happening there" ... then he can tell me everything that's happening, before it's happened.' Anthony is receiving important lessons from his mother on how to read and make sense of a story, and about the importance of anticipating what comes next. He knows implicitly that as listener he is actively involved in making sense of the words on the page, with his mother as guide. He knows too that the illustrations can help him to understand the story more fully, and is already skilled at matching meanings across the words and the pictures. 'You can't just read to him,' his mother explains, 'you've got to hold the book so he can see the pictures.'

Anthony's best-loved story is *Little Red Riding Hood* and somehow he has managed to acquire three versions of the tale, and knows parts of each by heart. He asks for the story to be read to him over and over again; it's clearly very powerful for him in some way. One evening his mother read him one of the versions of the story. Her reading took about seven minutes, and she paused once midway through the book to ask Anthony some questions. Then she read to the end:

MOTHER: 'Little Red Riding Hood's father took her by the hand and led her thankfully back to her mother, and how happy she was that things had turned out so well. "As long as I live," said Little Red Riding Hood, "I shall never leave the forest path when you have warned me not to do so." '

At the end of the reading Anthony's mother asks him a question which is designed to see if he has understood Red Riding Hood's error of judgement:

MOTHER: So what did she do wrong?
ANTHONY: Met a bad wolf.

She then rehearses with him the part the wolf played in events:

MOTHER: Yes. What did the wolf do?
ANTHONY: Ate her up.
MOTHER: And what did the wolf do to Grandmother?
ANTHONY: He ate her up too.

Anthony is not sure about the answer to the next question, perhaps because of the way it is phrased, so his mother rewords it, making the sense clearer for him:

MOTHER: Yeah. And who saved them both?
ANTHONY: Erm ...
MOTHER: Whose father saved them?
ANTHONY: Little Red Riding Hood's.

Anthony's mother signals that they are nearing the end of the story by giving an evaluative comment on it and inventing a future for the participants:

MOTHER: Yes. Very good, isn't it? He saved them and they're still alive now, aren't they?
ANTHONY: Yeah.

She leaves Anthony the satisfaction of bringing evil to an end in the forest:

MOTHER: And what's happened to the wolf?
ANTHONY: Dead!

These questions are designed to check Anthony's understanding of the story. In asking them, his mother is implicitly telling him that the book carries meaning and this is what he should be attending to. The time Anthony's mother is prepared to set aside for this shared reading session shows him how much she values him as a learner, and he knows this. It is interesting to note that this story-reading session, including questioning, was approximately twelve minutes long, probably much longer than any other conversation time between mother and son. During the session, and others like it, he learns from his mother that books are important and enjoyable things to give his attention to. He also learns that comprehension is important and that there is a new language in books, a literary language that he does not meet in his everyday conversations; words like 'thankfully' and structures like 'how happy she was' and 'you have warned me not to do so' set the reading session apart from his ordinary conversation and give Anthony a feel for the language of books.

I know the story of *Little Red Riding Hood* is deep inside him when, six months after starting school, he dictates his own version:

> Once upon a time there was Little Red Riding Hood. She went into the woods and she met a big bad wolf. And he hurried on to the woods. He got there just in time. He pulled the latch and came in. He ate Grandmother in one mouthful. Little Red Riding Hood came in. She saw the door wide open. She went upstairs and said, 'Grandmother, what big eyes you have,' said Little Red Riding Hood and the bad wolf struggled out of bed and gobbled her up in one mouthful. And her daddy came to see Grandmother but it was the bad wolf. He seen a black thing popped out and that was Little Red Riding Hood's grandmother. He chopped him up.

There is no doubt that Anthony is a sophisticated narrator. His spoken version of the story has, in parts, the feel of the language of the book: 'he hurried on to the woods', 'he pulled the latch', 'the bad wolf struggled out of bed and gobbled her up in one mouthful'. This was something he already knew about when he came to school. The experience of being read to by his mother and sister and by nursery teachers, and the stories he has watched on television, have all helped him to learn more about how to handle narrative, both as listener and as teller.

At school his teacher notes that he enjoys listening to stories and making up fictional worlds for himself and his friends through play. Three weeks after starting school he and his friend Mark sit at a table playing with Lego. They are making Transformers with the pieces:

ANTHONY: Mine can change into something else. These couldn't fight us 'cos they were goodies and they could fly.

MARK: They have to go up, don't they?

ANTHONY: [takes wheels] Pretend these batter us ... mine's bashed up.

MARK: Mine still ain't broken.

ANTHONY: I'm coming to transform you.

MARK: I'm dead now. [throws Lego on the floor]

ANTHONY: You don't fall 'cos I go faster. You can't still kill me.
MARK: This is your last chance. The wheels killed me once but they can't kill me twice.

Anthony and Mark kept up this intense running commentary to support their game for fifteen minutes, planning and creating this fictional world with an ongoing narrative. They are clearly very good at using language to play 'Let's pretend', weaving their fantasy world around their Lego.

Anthony's teacher says he seems to enjoy listening to stories and poems with the rest of the class but never picks up a book to look at by himself, even when invited to and even though he can see other children doing this. Perhaps this is because he is read to a lot at home and still has little experience of handling books by himself. He certainly seems to need someone with him while he reads, someone to help create and sustain that storyworld inside the book. At the same time he does seem to enjoy and learn from shared book-reading sessions with his teacher. Here, he and Reid look through a poetry book with their teacher, at her suggestion, and decide to read 'The Toaster'. This poem has the quality of a modern riddle and the boys have listened to their teacher read it several times to the class. Anthony can recall a little of the poetic language even before his teacher begins reading now. As he looks at the illustration he says: 'with jaws flaming ...'. His teacher affirms that he is right and then begins to read the poem. Anthony echoes her reading and both children join in when they feel confident:

TEACHER: Yes. 'A silver-*scaled dragon*'
ANTHONY: *scaled dragon*
TEACHER: 'with *jaws flaming red*'
ANTHONY: *jaws flaming red*
TEACHER: 'sits at my *elbow*'
ANTHONY: *elbow*
REID: *elbow*
TEACHER: 'and'
ANTHONY: toasted my *bread*
REID: *bread*
TEACHER: 'I *hand him fat slices*'
ANTHONY: *hand him fat slices*
REID: *slices*

Perhaps Reid's paraphrasing of the next line prompts Anthony to enjoy guessing what the silver-scaled dragon is all over again:

REID: One by one when they done he handed them back ...
ANTHONY: A pop-up toaster!

He knows this already, of course, because his teacher has read and
discussed the poem with the class before, but there is a satisfaction
nevertheless in guessing correctly all over again, and in knowing that you
are right. Anthony's teacher celebrates this with him, and makes a game
of his reading for him:

TEACHER: That's right. It is a pop-up toaster, isn't it?

When Anthony and Reid share *Mr Gumpy's Outing* with their teacher,
they are again on familiar territory because she has already read it to the
class several times. In spite of this, the questions Anthony asks his
teacher are those of an inexperienced reader still learning to find his way
through a storybook, and I recall that his mother has always held the
book while they read together, showing him the illustrations on request.
As they look at the title page, Anthony asks:

ANTHONY: Is this the beginning?
TEACHER: No. That tells us the title, look, 'Mr Gumpy's Outing'. And that's
    the name of the man who wrote it. John Burningham.
ANTHONY: Is this the end? [pointing to the next page with no words written
    on]
TEACHER: No. We have to turn over another page to find the beginning.

And so Anthony receives some reading lessons from his teacher about
how a book works, and about the concept of authorship. She has shown
him what a title is, she has told him that the book has been written by
a person, John Burningham, and pointed to where his name appears.
Then she explains that they will have to turn over to find out what the
story is about. Anthony watches as she turns the page:

TEACHER: 'Mr Gumpy owned a boat and his house was by a river.' Would
    you like to live in a house like Mr Gumpy's?
REID: That?
TEACHER: Mmm. By the river?
REID: No.
TEACHER: Wouldn't you? Why not?
ANTHONY: Too many animals might jump around and I might fall in the river
    and I can't swim.

Anthony has heard this story before and knows the central event. His 'I might fall in the river and I can't swim' shows him placing himself at the centre of the fiction, merging with the character of the little boy in the story, anticipating his plight as if it were his own, and perhaps indicating his own fear of water. His teacher's question has given him the chance to build this framework for understanding the story and to explain why it would not be a good idea to live by a river. Later in the story Anthony shows that he knows the text well enough to take over the reading from his teacher:

TEACHER: 'May I join you, Mr Gumpy? said the *goat*'
ANTHONY: *goat*. But don't kick.

His teacher supports him by telling him he is right and he enjoys predicting what will happen next:

TEACHER: That's right. He mustn't kick.
ANTHONY: He's going to kick.

Anthony's story-reading sessions with his teacher present him with a somewhat different experience from those offered by his mother. At home it is his mother who reads and remakes the story through her questions; at school Anthony is expected to take a greater part in developing the story through conversation. It would be wrong, though, to imagine that at home he is simply a passive listener when his mother reads to him. He is all the time making meanings for himself and his mother makes sure he attends to those meanings through her questions. This experience has made it possible for him to respond to stories at school by using judgement and reasoning. Here he discusses part of *Mr Gumpy's Outing* with Reid and their teacher and together they build a shared meaning for the text. Not only does Anthony use his feelings and judgements about characters – 'he shouldn't have let them in' – he is also learning to make sense of the meaning contained in the book by relating it to his knowledge of the world:

TEACHER: 'and into the water they fell.'
ANTHONY: Splash!
REID: Splash went the boat.
ANTHONY: It was a big boat that was. He shouldn't have let them in.
TEACHER: I hope they could all swim.
ANTHONY: I think so.
REID: The cat won't be able to.

TEACHER: Won't it?
REID: No.
ANTHONY: Cats can't swim.

'Cats can't swim,' says Anthony, and in making this firm statement he moves from the single incident in the book to a generalisation about all the cats in the world. His knowledge about cats may be at fault, but that is not at issue here. What is important is that he has justified Reid's comment, 'the cat won't be able to', by taking an intellectual leap from the particular to the general; he anticipates what might happen to the cat in the storyworld by relating the event to his knowledge of cats in the real world, and in this act we see his growing understanding of the concept of causality. Learning to read for Anthony is not only developing into a new way of understanding texts. It is also becoming a means of developing abstract thought processes.

Anthony was already an experienced narrator when he came to school, and this is demonstrated in his reading of *The Elephant and the Bad Baby* four weeks after he started. He uses his knowledge of narrative form, his memory of the language of the story and the cues from the illustrations to guide him through his own version of the story, which has already been read to him by his teacher. Here, he reads the first three pages. The actual text is shown in brackets:

> Once there was an elephant. (Once upon a time there was an elephant.)
>
> Once there was a little bad baby. (And one day the Elephant went for a walk and he met a Bad Baby. And the Elephant said to the Bad Baby, 'Would you like a ride?' And the Bad Baby said, 'Yes.')
>
> He said do you want a ride and the bad baby said yes. Went rumpeta, rumpeta, rumpeta all the way down the road. (So the Elephant stretched out his trunk, and picked up the Bad Baby and put him on his back, and they went rumpeta, rumpeta, rumpeta, all down the road.)

The following day Anthony drew a picture of the elephant with people beside him (Figure 6) and retold the main events of the story as he drew:

> It's all the people chasing after the elephant. Tick tock. A long trunk. That's the end. He never said please for the food. The elephant sat down and slided off and all the people bumped into him.

When Anthony had been in school for six months, something

Figure 6: It's all the people chasing after the elephant. Tick tock. A long trunk. That's the end. He never said please for the food. The elephant sat down and slided off and all the people bumped into him.

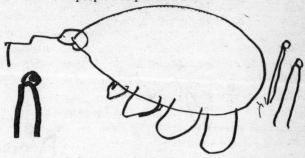

happened that may explain his strong response to *Little Red Riding Hood*. Apparently he was watching the video of *Jaws* on television most Saturday mornings at the time, and he told me this story about himself and a shark as he drew a picture (Figure 7):

That's me. Well, I've been doing a lot of fishing. I went fishing. A shark came up and it bit me right here where it's all swollen. [He pointed to a part of himself on the picture.] My dad put a bomb in its mouth and it blowed all to pieces. Going to put a bomb in his mouth and it blowed up. All the tooth came up one by one by one and I picked them up and I threw the teeth away in the bin and all the blood came up. And I seen the belly come up.

Anthony is 'storying', adapting the story of the film for his own purposes. His power as a narrator allows him to insert this intensely personal fictionalised account of himself going fishing, being caught by the shark and then rescued by his father, into the violent images he recalls from *Jaws*. In so doing he transforms terrifying events into a satisfying experience with a happy ending for himself. The story seems to meet some inexpressible need in him, and the comparison with *Little Red Riding Hood* is striking; in both this shark story and in *Little Red Riding Hood* a child is eaten by a savage beast, the wolf or the shark – metaphors for all that is dark and terrifying – and saved at the last minute by a courageous father. I believe this echoes meanings in Anthony's own

Figure 7: That's me. Well, I've been doing a lot of fishing.
A shark came up and it bit me right here where it's all
swollen. My dad put a bomb in its mouth and it blowed all
to pieces. Going to put a bomb in his mouth and it blowed
up. All the tooth came up one by one and I picked them up
and I threw the teeth away in the bin and all the blood
came up. And I seen the belly come up.

The shark bit me

This is the shark what bit me

life. He doesn't actually live with his father, though he sees him from
time to time, and he may be using the power of story to help him to
consider his own future, hypothesising about an idealised relationship
with his father, who will be there to make things safe for him.

After two terms in school Anthony is controlling the pace of his own
literacy learning, with support from home and school. Stories are
centrally important to him in this enterprise, both those he reads and
those he tells. While he is still a young and inexperienced reader, he is
a successful apprentice and has already learned a good deal about reading
and writing from his early encounters with print. Stories are a way of
giving him pleasure, whether they're in books or on television, and his
attempt to understand them in terms of his own life clearly involve him
in levels of comprehension that go far beyond enjoyment.

Anthony's reading experience is growing; before he came to school he already knew about stories (in books and on television), poems, newspapers, shopping lists, labels and titles. He had seen books treated with care and noted his mother's and his sister's respect for literacy. At school now he has no difficulty in using story to support his own fantasy games, or to script a hypothetical future for himself. He sees around him in his classroom that same respect for literacy learning that he sees at home and begins to ask questions about the way a book is set out. His own path towards literacy has been defined, by home and by school, and in one sense the way ahead is clear; yet I cannot help but think that Anthony will take a hand in defining the route for himself as he takes the next steps on the road to becoming a reader.

4

Geeta

Geeta came into school cheerfully with her mother on her first morning. She wore a smart dress, as her mother wished, rather than the trousers she would really have preferred, and her long black hair was carefully plaited. Geeta confidently looked around for things to do and children she already knew. She had spent a year in a nursery school and knew what to expect when she came into the classroom at school: pictures on the wall, tables set out with Lego, paper and paints and crayons, and a corner with dressing-up clothes. She was used to choosing her own activities and at her nursery, after 'family time' in the morning, she would occupy herself with different tasks until dinner time without ever needing to go to see her teacher. Indeed, when I watched her playing in the nursery I saw a little girl who seemed very much at ease and totally confident, sitting at a table with six other children, five boys and one girl, building a tower block with Lego. She held centre-stage, and was making the children laugh by knocking each block off one at a time against her nose.

Geeta's parents welcomed me warmly when I went to see them in their modern detached house, which is in a street of mainly older terraced housing towards the centre of town. We walked through the entrance hall into the front room, furnished with a modern three-piece suite, coffee table and music centre and plants. A large photograph of Geeta's grandfather stands on the fireplace and beside it is a photograph of the family's spiritual leader, Maharaj Charan Singh. A pair of large, silvered giraffes stands elegantly at each end of the fireplace; Geeta's mother brought them back from India on her last visit. Angela, the eldest daughter, brings us tea and biscuits. Her father wears a suit and her mother is dressed in a shulwar kamiz; she's slim and delicately featured and complains of tiredness. Geeta comes to sit by me and we begin to talk about their aspirations for their children.

Geeta's parents believe that their children should be well educated, and are willing to spend time and money to give them the best opportunities they can afford. They decided to send Geeta to a nursery because they felt she should 'sit down and learn and mix with other children' before she came to school. They feel that Geeta is clever and are ambitious for her, as they are for her two older sisters and older brother, all now at secondary schools in the city. Also, they are fully occupied in running their factory where they manufacture shirts and blouses, and they knew they would not be able to give Geeta as many different experiences at home as she would receive in a nursery.

Even so, as the youngest child Geeta is 'treated like the baby in the family', says her mother, and given a great deal of attention. 'Everyone knows her name,' her mother adds, 'even the shopkeepers.' But she is particularly close to the mother, who describes their mutually warm and supportive relationship like this:

> She is that close to me she even sleeps with me at night. I never love any other child like I do with her. I don't know why I felt like it, to be with her all the time ... she still sleeps with me, one arm on top of my neck and the other under my neck. If I want to turn this side, she will turn before me; even if she's asleep, deep asleep, she will wake up.

Long before Geeta came to school she took herself seriously as a reader and had witnessed and joined in with a variety of reading and writing activities at home and at nursery school. At four and a half, about to enter school for the first time, she is already aware of the importance of reading and writing in the lives of people in her family; her older sisters and brother unconsciously model book-reading and writing behaviour for her as she watches them doing their homework, and their attention to the literacy of their schools also shows her a way to future school success of her own. She observes them writing essays and notes and reading textbooks as they do their homework and she sometimes writes or draws alongside them; she sees her father writing letters, working on his accounts, making notes, consulting the telephone directory; and she sees him reading holy books. She sees her mother and sister reading for pleasure, and at night Geeta and her mother read together in bed: 'If I go to bed at nine or nine-thirty I read a book, or a letter, or a women's magazine, or an Indian newspaper, and Geeta will take her own book,' her mother explains. Geeta accompanies Ranu, her eleven-year-old sister, to the library, and chooses books. 'She doesn't know the ABC but she still brings a book,' her mother says. And it's Ranu who spends most time reading with her small sister. 'She's the only one in the family who's got the time to,' says her mother. 'You see, she doesn't have as much homework as the others.' Angela reads with Geeta sometimes and tells me that Geeta 'tries to read according to the pictures'.

Geeta also reads birthday cards and wedding invitations when they arrive and she watches advertisements on television, especially her favourite, the one for 'Care Bears'. Sometimes the family watch Indian films together on video, and Geeta enjoys cartoons too.

Her mother was twelve or thirteen when she came to England and she recalls trying to learn English. 'I didn't even know the ABC,' she explains. She was taught English at school and now reads and writes in both English and Punjabi. She remembers her parents reading from the holy books, her mother and grandfather reading newspapers and her father reading novels. In the Punjab on warm nights her family slept on the flat roof of their house and listened to stories: 'Some were so long they lasted many nights,' she remembers. Geeta's father recalls similar experiences, and although these storytelling events are now a part of their history the family's inherited need for a time to be close together and to share cultural and religious experiences has endured and is fulfilled each day through their religious observances. At half-past eight each evening incense is lit, and the family pray together. Sometimes one member reads from a prayer book; at another time 'if you know the right words you don't have to open the book'. Afterwards, the book is respectfully covered with a cloth. The next morning, after washing or bathing, the cover is carefully removed. The family share a set of religious practices and beliefs set down in a book called *The Master Answers* (1966). This contains the teachings of Maharaj Charan Singh, who advocates a life of hard work, self-discipline and meditation, in order to find inner peace with God. Sometimes the family visit the Hindu temple if there is a particular festival they want to observe; but since they feel that God is everywhere around them they often choose to pray and meditate at home. I was invited to look through their prayer book. It is a weighty volume, bound in leather and written in Punjabi.

There are photographs in it of different spiritual leaders and illustrations from Hindu stories. Geeta looked at the prayer book as I turned the pages and recognised an illustration of Rama and Sita. She is not allowed to touch the book until she is older, although she did try to turn the pages as I held it and was reprimanded.

At nursery Geeta's interest in books and stories was fostered by her teacher and *John Brown, Rose and the Midnight Cat* and *The Very Hungry Caterpillar* became her favourite picture-story books. She was also encouraged to make writing patterns and to recognise her namecard as it was held up. Her teacher remarked that she 'didn't have much interest in writing, but she liked drawing'. I watched her one day in the nursery as she drew a figure which she said was 'Daddy' (Figure 8). I asked Geeta to 'make it say Daddy in letters' and she wrote above her drawing. Her writing is a mixture of signs, some little figures, and a capital G, third from the right. 'That's my name,' she said, and pointed to the G. She already knows that writing has a symbolic function, that it stands for something else, and she is able to invent writing by inventing symbols for names. In this case, the symbols stand for 'Daddy'. This business of naming is crucially important to Geeta; learning to name things and people, to say names, to write them, is to have control over them, to know them in a new way – and, central to all this, learning to make the letters of her own name, to see the G in front of her, to be able to read it, gives her a new control over language and an identity as a language user.

Three months before Geeta comes to school, she and I read *Not Now Bernard* together. Her nursery teacher had told me she knew and enjoyed the story. We sat side by side on the settee and as I read she attended closely, repeating my phrases and sometimes using them as cues to help her guess what came next, taking the reading on from me. It is worth remembering that Geeta is using her second language in this and subsequent extracts:

HM: 'Hello, Mum.'
GEETA: 'Hello, Mum. Not Now Bernard.'

She was clearly familiar with the story:

HM: Who did he meet in the garden?
GEETA: A monster.
HM: And what did he say to the monster?

Figure 8: Daddy

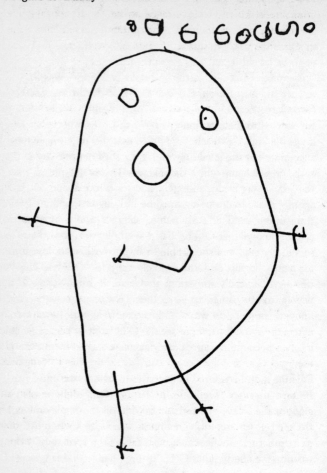

GEETA: Hello, Monster.
HM: Hello, Monster. And what did the Monster do?
GEETA: Eat all up.
HM: Every bit of him.
GEETA: Every bit of him.

Geeta's eyes ranged over the illustrations as we spoke, just as Angela had
noted, confirming for me how centrally important illustrations are in

assisting young children's understanding of a story. She often commented skilfully and creatively on the pictures in the book, making a sequence of events from what she saw. Here, for example, she comments on an illustration of Bernard's mother:

GEETA: She's got ... and she's watering the plants and she's wetting all the plants.

Geeta's close scrutiny of pictures helps her to make sense of a story in her own terms. She has learnt this from her story-telling sessions with Angela and her teachers at nursery school and from her early media literacy: watching television films and cartoons has shown her how to match visual clues with words in order to make a story. She will bring this knowledge and skill with her to her book-reading at school.

Later that same afternoon Geeta decided to draw the monster from the story (Figure 9). When she had completed the huge shape, she proceeded to draw some G's up the left-hand edge of the monster. She said these were 'my name'. She then drew some number 3's in the top left-hand corner, and some upside-down A's in the bottom corner opposite. Down the left-hand side she drew a long curly line, saying it was T, E and B. These letters are distributed randomly around her drawing, seeming to fill in the space. There is no linearity; she writes where she chooses to, using the letter and number shapes she knows. She seems to be at the stage of drawing letters and numbers; and drawing the letter G to stand for one word, her name, thus keeping herself quite literally at the centre of her own learning experience.

Once at school Geeta uses her storymaking skills to plan and create a fictional world for herself and her friends in the playhouse. She opens the dressing-up box with great gusto and dons a white hat, oblivious of all around her. She gives Sherine a handbag. First they decide on their roles and responsibilities:

SHERINE: Come on, Mum.
GEETA: I'm not Mum. We're two sisters.
SHERINE: You hold the dog. I'll have the baby [she gets a doll out of the box for herself and a toy dog for Geeta].
GEETA: We both have babies [she reaches in the box for another doll]. This is my baby and I'll have the dog too. I'm going to the park.

At this point they walk in celebratory fashion around the classroom,

Figure 9: **Geeta's drawing of a monster – and her writing**

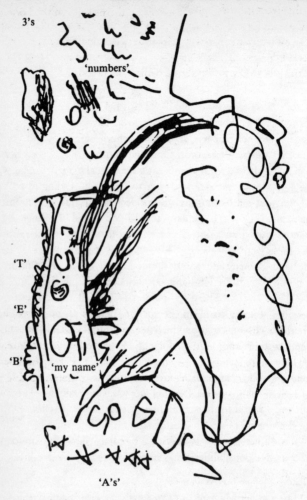

holding their babies and pulling the dog along behind them. Then they are joined by two more children and it is time, of course, for tea. Sherine and Geeta support each other in creating this make-believe world through their use of language to organise the story they invent for themselves. Geeta's mastery of narrative form enables her to do this

well, taking on the roles of both mother and sister and building a context
for the events to take place.

When Geeta had been at school for about three months she began to
ask questions about the way books are written and one day we had this
conversation about *The Snowman*, a book without a written text, where
the story is told entirely through the illustrations:

GEETA: What's that say? [pointing to the title]
HM: '*The Snowman*.'
GEETA: The Snowman. That's all said Snowman? [pointing to the title]
HM: And that says Raymond Briggs [pointing to his name].
GEETA: He wrote that?
HM: He wrote ... he made the pictures and it was his idea for the story.
GEETA: He wrote *The Snowman*? All of this?
HM: Mmm. He drew all the pictures for the book and he had the idea for the
   story.
GEETA: I haven't seen him.
HM: No. I've seen a picture of him but I've never seen him in real life.
GEETA: How did he make this, then?
HM: I think he had a good idea for a story, and he's a very good artist, and
   he started to draw all the pictures for the book.

Geeta is using her growing knowledge of language as an object, to be
used and manipulated, as she begins to grapple with the idea of stories
being invented, written by people. She is beginning, in other words, to
use language to talk about language. She offers her own retelling of *The
Snowman*, and tells me what she needs to do in order to be able to read
the story in her own words:

GEETA: *The Snowman* haven't got words. Just have to get some words.

In announcing this she becomes the re-creator and the authorial voice
for *The Snowman*, matching her own words with those of the
illustrations in the book:

There's a boy, he's gone to sleep and it's snowing and he just dress up and
he looking out the window. It's snowing and he pulls his boots on and go
outside and he left his hat off because he making a big ball a snowman. He
getting some nose and eyes and and mouth. He get the mouth, put it with
the finger in the mouth and he just nearly finished ...

In Geeta's head is the memory of a previous retelling, and she brings *The*

Snowman to life all over again by shaping the illustrations into a story with her language. I am her audience, and listen silently. She continues to tell the story in this fashion, looking perceptively at each illustration, until she reaches the end:

> ... so he's gone to seaside to fly away and he and snowman said oh and he came back home and he and he get out and he wake up and he couldn't sleep and he gone downstairs gone upstairs and downstairs. The snowman was melt.

Not long after this *The Jolly Postman* became one of Geeta's favourite books, and her shared reading of the book shows clearly what she knows about reading. We are sitting together looking at the page where the postman brings the letter from Goldilocks to the three bears:

GEETA: Three bears. One daddy one, one mummy one. We got three bears of that haven't we?

There are two things going on here. First, Geeta is looking closely at the illustration and recognises the three bears as the same bears she knows from the traditional fairy story. Then, she recalls that we have another book with the story of Goldilocks in; in other words, she is discovering that the three bears can appear in more than one version of a story, and still remain the same bears. I read what it says on the envelope:

HM: And it says 'Mr and Mrs Bear, Three Bears Cottage, The Woods.'
GEETA: 'The Woods.'

Geeta repeats 'The Woods' after me and waits for me to continue:

HM: ... and if you open it up ...
GEETA: Yeah ...
HM: It says –

Now Geeta takes over the reading and has a go at remembering what the letter says:

GEETA: Bear Cottages. Get for letter for dear three bears.

I help her out and continue reading. As I read she ghosts the words quietly and joins in with 'your house' and 'says':

HM: 'Dear Mr and Mrs Bear and baby bear. I am very sorry indeed that I came into *your house*'

GEETA: *your house*

HM: 'and ate baby bear's porridge. Mummy says I am a bad girl. I hardly eat any porridge when she cooks it she *says*'

GEETA: *says*

HM: Daddy says he will mend the little chair. Love from Goldilocks. PS. Baby Bear – '

Geeta interjects at this point. She seems to need me to stop while she makes sense of what has happened so far. She returns to the illustrations again:

GEETA: That's the daddy one that's the mummy one the baby one [pointing to three bowls of jelly on Goldilocks's letter]. Where she's coming sunshine and sky up there [pointing to the picture of the sun and sky on Goldilocks's letter].

Then Geeta goes on to do something new; she pays attention to an individual word on the page:

GEETA: ... and there's a like ... a like somewhere. I saw it here.

I ask her to clarify what she means:

HM: Like. You mean the word 'like'?

GEETA: Like.

HM: Like?

GEETA: I and like.

I scan the text for 'like' and find 'likes'. I point to it:

HM: There's 'likes'.

GEETA: Yeah, oh yeah.

And so we have a conversation about the book on two levels; there's the story itself that we remake together, with its networks into other stories Geeta knows, and there's the conversation about the words on the page, which we discuss using specialised language ourselves.

Geeta does not read at home with her parents. They are extremely busy running their factory and feel, in any case, that if she needs help then her older brother and sisters will be there to assist her. Here, Ranu and Geeta read *Little Red Riding Hood* together at home, into a tape-recorder. Geeta, in fact, does most of the storytelling and Ranu supports her by whispering a word or phrase if she hesitates, thus ensuring that Geeta's retelling sounds fluent, effortless and uncorrected. Because she is supported in this way, Geeta is exuberant and inventive. Here is part of her retelling:

GEETA: Goodbye, says Red Riding Hood's mummy. If you saw your daddy, if that Big Bad Wolf gets you tell your daddy to come back for tea. Little Red Riding Hood said to her grandmother which flowers she likes.

I sense that Ranu is slightly uncomfortable with Geeta's interpretation of the story and would prefer her to try and read the actual words, so she brings Geeta back to the text. Geeta repeats the words after her but then continues with her own retelling:

RANU: 'Little Red Riding Hood sees some trees.'
GEETA: Little Red Riding Hood sees some trees and some flowers. She said grandmother likes flowers.

Ranu whispers the text to her again, very quietly, but the words of the text are not what Geeta needs at this moment. The version of the story she wants is in her head, along with some of the literary language she has remembered from previous tellings:

GEETA: I can make up this to read. She see up to the ... she see the big bad wolf and he near a tree. He said play with me. Play with me. I can't. I can't. I have to see the grandmother. Erm ... I got cakes and flowers for Grandmother.

Ranu seems to accept Geeta's version and now sensitively corrects her when individual words change the meaning for her:

GEETA: I see ... the wolf gets ...
RANU: goes ...
GEETA: goes to Grandmother's ...
RANU: home ...
GEETA: home. Grandmother. Knock. Knock. Grandmother. Knock. Knock. Little Red Riding Hood. Come in she says. She sees the big bad wolf. She gets to the ...
RANU: cupboard ...
GEETA: cupboard. Help. Help. What she says?

The two girls continue in this fashion until they reach the end of the story. Geeta is so enthusiastic, so much in control of the way she wants to put her version of the story across, that Ranu has to be quick and clever to anticipate her needs, though I sense she is frustrated by Geeta's lack of attention to the text itself. At school Geeta's teacher is not frustrated in this way: her experience has shown her that Geeta's early responses are very much a part of the process of learning to read. She tries to meet Geeta's reading needs as she shares a book with her, attending to all her queries and setting up a comfortable reading context where Geeta feels at ease to ask about anything that might be puzzling her. Her teacher begins by introducing the book:

TEACHER: *The Noisiest Class in School.* By Pauline Hill.
GEETA: Pauline Hill.
TEACHER: That's Pauline Hill wrote the words in the book, wrote the story.
GEETA: All the pictures?
TEACHER: No. The pictures, the illustrations, were by Joan Beales.
GEETA: Joan Beales.
TEACHER: That's another lady.
GEETA: That's another lady.
TEACHER: It is, yes.
GEETA: Who drew the pictures?
TEACHER: Joan Beales.
GEETA: Joan Beales.
TEACHER: That's right. Go on then. You turn the next page over.

She hands the book over to Geeta and, as her teacher reads, Geeta listens carefully. She wants an explanation for everything she doesn't understand, working in collaboration with her teacher to make meaning from the text. Here, she worries away at the word 'tatty' in order to discover its meaning:

TEACHER: 'Dirty Bert, with his tatty shirt – '
GEETA: What does tatty mean?
TEACHER: Tatty? Untidy. Not very nice.
GEETA: Not very nice?
TEACHER: A bit ripped, might be, tatty. Or a bit creased.
GEETA: Like this? [looking at her own blouse]
TEACHER: A bit creased like that, yes. But that isn't really tatty. That's creased because you've been wearing it all day.

Satisfied that she understands a little of what 'tatty' means, Geeta's teacher begins to read the next page, where she finds that Geeta responds to the information in the story by matching it against her own experience in order to make sense of it. Just as she used the example of her own blouse to enlarge her meaning of the word 'tatty', she has the skill to find a way of matching other incidents in the book to her own experience:

TEACHER: 'Our school has got a bus. It picks us all up each morning and takes us to school.'

GEETA: My dad goes to the factory and my mum, and she come back to fetch me and goes back to the factory to eat her dinner.

Geeta's teacher could have continued reading at this point, but instead she elicits more information from Geeta in order to help her to understand the text more fully:

TEACHER: She has her dinner at the factory?

GEETA: No, she brings her dinner at the factory 'cos we haven't got no dinners at the factory. We just got the coffee. We still haven't got any coffee, right. We got the machine of it so we got a new one. We got an old one, it's broken. It doesn't work for six months.

This shared book-reading shows clearly that the meaning does not lie in the printed words alone; indeed, meaning has to be brought to life by Geeta as she searches for experiences in her own life that shed light on her understanding of the story. Geeta matches her own experiences against those of the children in the story, and in so doing makes sense of both her own world and the world of the book. The story about the broken coffee machine, from her own world, helps her to make sense of her mother's experience at work. Geeta's teacher allows her the time to tussle with the meaning of each page in this fashion. Further on in the story, on a page that shows the children in the story painting, Geeta pays attention to two elements of a picture-story book that we know are important to her: the illustrations and the words and letters. She finds a way of attending to both, assisted by her teacher:

TEACHER: 'Do you like painting? Our class does.'

GEETA: We do paintings. We do paintings. He's got a nice one, she's got a nice one [pointing to the paintings].

TEACHER: They've all written their names on the paintings.

GEETA: Looks like my name up there [pointing to 'Gene'].

TEACHER: Yes. Your name begins with that letter.

GEETA: Yes. You've got two of those in your name [pointing to the two 'e's' in 'Gene'].

TEACHER: Yes. A 'G' and two 'e's'. Gene's got a 'G' and two 'e's' in his name.

Geeta could not read this book without the help of her teacher, who makes the author's words available to her by reading them aloud and then makes it possible for Geeta to respond to the reading in this active way. Geeta interrogates every page in the book, and in so doing learns to establish connections between her own first-hand experience and the experience she comes across in the story, something she must continue to do in her head when she is a silent, independent reader. I am continually impressed by Geeta's ability to collaborate with someone else in order to make sense of what she is reading. She seems to know intuitively how and when she needs to do this, and the kinds of questions she needs to ask in order to move her understanding forward and stay in control of her own learning.

As I observe Geeta I see a child in control of her own language learning, who is intensely curious about things she doesn't understand and knows how to use adults to help her gain information. These observations suggest that Geeta is well on her way to becoming a reader, even though she has yet to achieve mastery of the alphabetic nature of written language. Her conscious awareness of herself as a language user, and of language itself as an object for discussion and use, are evidence of the high expectations she has of herself. She talks about language and about herself as a language user constantly – 'The Snowman haven't got no words', 'when I'm big I'll write a sentence', 'that's like my name'; and she is interested in recognising words when she is reading: 'there's a like a like somewhere'.

Geeta is moving to a point in her language development where she is paying attention to meaning and at the same time making connections for herself about language and about the form books take. Her approach to literacy was shaped before she came to school by the social practices of her home, and there is little doubt that she wants to be as successful as her brother and sisters. The particular social and literacy patterns of her home, her familiarity with books, her interest in story and pictures, her encounters with religious literacy, underlie her early reading experiences and help me to understand the high expectations she has of herself as a future reader and writer.

5

Reid

'I'm good at writing,' Reid said, four weeks after he started school; 'if someone showed me how to write. I can do number 4's.' Reid told me this as he drew a picture and watched me making notes by his side. What he said about himself is important: it reflects his confidence in himself as a learner and the expectation that he can and will learn from someone who knows more than he does. This attitude is firmly embedded in the kinds of learning that happen in his home, where Reid is involved in learning things from his parents and older brother and sister.

Reid's parents believe that school provides their children with the values and attitudes conducive to hard work and success. They hold strong beliefs about how learning can be fostered in their home and make every effort to provide a stimulating environment for their children to grow up in. Their cultural assumptions match those of schools and their views are familiar and similar to those held by many professional educationalists. 'We look for the learning potential in everything,' Reid's mother explains. 'We believe in spending time constructively and creatively as a way of preparing the children for life.' They feel that Reid had already had 'quite a varied sort of experience of life' and have taken him to the seaside, zoos and bird sanctuaries, to museums, antique fairs and insect fairs. The family go ice skating and swimming and regularly visit friends and relations. Reid's mother even exploits the learning opportunities which a shoppping trip affords: 'I see it as a special time for Reid to be with me on my own, just mother and son together. I did the same with Amber when she was smaller. I get Reid to feel as if he's part of the expedition, and quite an important part as well.' She might ask him to choose a packet of biscuits, but it has to be 'a sort we all like, so he's got to think about it'. In this way she encourages his sense of social responsibility towards the rest of the family.

Reid lives in a large ivy-covered Edwardian cottage in Hall Green on the north-east boundary of the city. It isn't in the school's catchment area, but when the family moved house a few years ago they requested that the children should stay at their present school. They have worked hard to make the cottage comfortable and aesthetically pleasing, collecting antiques and designing colour schemes and furnishings with care, and planning the cottage garden.

In the household everyone's interests are fostered and supported, talked about and shared. Reid's father, a precision engineer by trade, loves anything to do with the natural world, and insects in particular. 'It's something I never grew out of,' he says. 'I'm like a child.' He has an impressive collection of insects in a polished Victorian cabinet, all carefully labelled and documented. The family watch nature programmes together on television, and on holiday they pick and identify flowers, go 'rock-pooling', collect skulls, watch birds, and help each other to use information books and field guides to identify what they see and collect. 'It's bred into them to enjoy the nature side of it,' Reid's father explains. His other passion is for Frank Zappa. He keeps a scrapbook about the singer and owns every album he has made. He once wrote to the singer, telling him that Reid's second name is Zappa and enclosing a copy of his birth certificate with photos and information about the family. He is still disappointed that Frank Zappa never replied.

I visit Reid's home at about eight o'clock in the evening, so that Reid's mother has had time to make sure the children are in bed. We sit in the lounge to talk. It's a cosy room, furnished with easy chairs, a music centre and a television. There's an aquarium in an alcove and records and tapes are stored on shelves. Reid's mother is a trained nursery nurse and works in a school for handicapped children. Last year she studied A level English in her own time and for her own interest, and she is considering taking a teacher training course. She also paints, etches and once wrote a children's story. She also wrote a book of poems and dedicated them to Liam, her eldest son. She loves poetry and 'sometimes as we're going along in the car, if something triggers it off, I suddenly start bursting into Thomas Love Peacock or Wilfred Owen or something! I've always loved to repeat poems. I can repeat nearly every poem I've ever had to learn.'

Literacy for Reid is embedded in daily ways of living. He sees an unusually wide variety of reading and writing around him in his home, and is invited to share in a good deal of this. He observes his parents and older brother and sister reading and writing for various purposes and in different ways. Books are inseparable from the life of the family and are accorded high status within the household. Pinned to a board in the kitchen are bills that need paying, pools coupons, lists of jobs to do, invitations to parties or weddings, E additive and diet sheets and tickets for dances or concerts. There's a kitchen calendar where Reid's mother jots down reminders about birthdays, dentist's appointments, and so on. The kitchen drawers are filled with writing paper and envelopes, cards to send, address and telephone books, club books and an Argos catalogue, and all the paperwork for the mail order club. Reid's mother also keeps an exercise book in which she's written an extended shopping list of 'every single thing we ever use', and she uses this as a checklist. In addition, she writes at least two letters a week and one full page in her diary every day. Reid has always been encouraged to write for himself; he writes his own name on birthday cards and sends off for things on cereal packets. In return, he receives birthday cards and parcels addressed to him containing, for instance, tennis balls from a Start packet, or tapes from a Weetabix cereal box. In the car there is a list of car numbers of stolen cars, taken from the *Coventry Evening Telegraph*, and the family look at number plates as they drive along, hoping to spot a stolen car. Maps and caravan handbooks and holiday brochures are also kept in the car and caravan.

All the children have their own bedroom, and each room upstairs has its own bookshelves. In their cottage there has been space to make one of their upstairs rooms into a library, with a large comfortable settee, bookshelves, books, posters, games, toys in boxes, pinboarding, certificates and engraved trophies. The family go to book sales at the local library and 'we clean the library out usually'. The children keep some books in their own bedrooms but are encouraged to keep their books in the upstairs library so that they remain in good condition. Reid's father describes himself as a bookworm: 'I think reading's terrific,' he says, 'Franz Kafka. Trying to read all through that. Heavy going, but good. Science fiction. Tolkien. Got them all. Nature, butterfly books. Reference books. Got them all.' When he was a boy he had his own library: 'I've still got some of the books,' he says. 'I used to put numbers in them and sit at a little desk and lend them out to people with a little ticket.' Reid's mother loves Shakespeare and poetry and enjoyed some of the novels she read for English A level, but mostly she reads non-fiction works, usually to do with different handicaps in connection with her work; she is also interested in the Second World War.

Reid, then, is growing up in an environment where reading and writing are central to the way the family lives. 'Right from when he was small there's always been so many books about that he's always felt at home with books,' says his mother. In the upstairs library he has watched Amber, aged seven, browsing through books, and now spends time doing this himself. Sometimes all three children go to this special room and sit on the settee with a pile of books each. As well as choosing picture-story books, Reid likes to read his brother's dinosaur books or his father's butterfly or insect books. In the public library, too, Reid chooses his own books. 'We make it an enjoyable experience for them and they sit on the little chairs and look through the books,' his mother says.

Reid also begins to understand a little of the story of his own life and his family's own history, as he looks through the family photograph album with his parents. 'You tell stories of their life really,' his parents explain as his mother shows him photographs of relations and of herself as a little girl. In this way Reid learns to make sense of the passage of time, learns that he has a past and his mother has too, as he finds a place for himself in his family's history.

Reid's parents both feel that it is important for the children to have a bedtime story. Their own happy memories of being read to as children make this an activity they want their children to share. 'My mum used to take me in her bed at night and read or tell me a story about when she was a little girl,' Reid's mother explains. His father also has a memory of shared stories: 'Dad was mad on telling me stories. I can remember always getting told a story,' he says, and now he reads or tells a bedtime story to Reid and Amber every night. While Reid is waiting for his father to finish reading to Amber, he sometimes sits in bed and looks at a book by himself, and he may carry on looking at a book when his father has finished reading to him. Sometimes he chooses the book to be read; sometimes his father chooses, and occasionally makes up a story for Reid and Amber: 'I usually have them two in it.' At times Reid enjoys the same book over and over again: 'When he was two he wanted *Good Morning Baby Bear*, oh God, every single night!' his mother remembers.

When Reid shares a book with his parents he is encouraged to enter into the kind of interactive dialogue that his parents feel will help him understand the story. Before he came to school he was sharing picture-story books regularly with his mother. Here, three months before Reid is due to come to school, they read *That Fat Cat* together. This book belongs to the family and Reid has heard it before. They are in the front room, because this is where the tape-recorder is, though normally Reid would read upstairs with his mother. She begins by letting him try to recall the title:

MOTHER: Do you know what this book's called?
REID: Yes, the cat got stuck in ...

She acknowledges his attempt and begins to read to him:

MOTHER: *That Fat Cat* it's called. So you were nearly right, weren't you? 'Once upon a time there was a big fat cat, called Kafka. He was very lazy. What he liked to do best was to sit in front of the fire and sleep. And when he wasn't sleeping he liked to eat. He ate two big cans of cat food every day, and drank three saucers of milk.'

Reid interjects as she finishes the page:

REID: Mum, can I have a swim in my pool when it's warm?

Reid has not long come back from swimming with his father and this surely prompts his remark, which is quite unconnected with the story. Perhaps he is trying to divert his mother's attention away from the reading, somehow needing to keep a foothold in the real world, firmly resisting the world of the book. His mother allows this diversion, and has to work hard to try and understand him as he goes on to say:

REID: Toys used to be in there.
MOTHER: Used to be in where?
REID: The swimming bath.
MOTHER: What? In town?
REID: What?
MOTHER: In town. The swimming baths in town where you've just been?
REID: Yes. Well, toys used to be in the swimming baths.
MOTHER: I don't remember. What sort of toys?
REID: Well, boats. Small boats.
MOTHER: Was there?
REID: Yeah.
MOTHER: I don't remember.

REID: When I went there, when I went there I saw some toys there.
MOTHER: Did you? Right then. Shall we carry on with the story now?

Reid's mother isn't sure what he is trying to tell her and she asks him a series of questions to help make his meaning clear. This conversation exemplifies the way in which she respects and values his talk, even though it does not seem to have any relevance to the task in hand. When the time seems right, she takes Reid back to the book. As she reads, she pauses every so often to ask him questions about the text in order to find out if he's understood it:

MOTHER: 'So the next day, Daddy gave Kafka just half a tin of cat food and one saucer of milk.' Do you think he'd be very happy about that?
REID: No.
MOTHER: Why?
REID: 'Cos he wants to eat he wants to have loads.

She takes this opportunity to help Reid match his knowledge of the story to his memory of his favourite foods, thus bringing the story world and his own world closer together, to help him understand the feelings of the cat in the story:

MOTHER: He wants to have loads and loads. A bit like you then isn't he, really?
REID: No.
MOTHER: Oh well, you have loads and loads of dinner, don't you?
REID: I don't have loads and loads of ice cream.
MOTHER: Don't you? You're always saying to me ... what do you say?
REID: I want a sweetie!
MOTHER: So you're a bit like Kafka. You might get fat like him if you eat like you do.

Reid's mother helps him to anticipate what will happen next in the story:

MOTHER: ... 'but when he tries to get out of the flap' ...
REID: ... He couldn't get out.
MOTHER: ... 'he was stuck tight.'

Later on in the story, the name of one of the child characters takes Reid's mother into a conversation with Reid about his auntie. She initiates the discussion and takes Reid out of the text while they talk about their family together:

MOTHER: 'So Granny called the children.' Do you remember their names?

REID: Tim and ... erm ... Jane.
MOTHER: Yes. That's like my sister, isn't it, Jane?
REID: Yes.
MOTHER: Where does Jane live?
REID: Jane lives a long way away.
MOTHER: A long way away ... and who lives with Jane?
REID: Gary.
MOTHER: ... and ... you've forgotten somebody. Jane, Gary and little ...
REID: Lois.
MOTHER: Lois, that's right.

Mention of the baby brings this comment from Reid:

REID: I wish we had a baby.

His mother acknowledges his comment and reminds Reid that Lois did
come to stay with them. Reid misunderstands her reply; if there was a
baby in the house it must have been when he or Amber was a baby:

MOTHER: Do you? Well, we did have her for one night, didn't we?
REID: Yes. That was me and Amber being the baby.

His mother realises he has misunderstood and attempts to help him:

MOTHER: No. We had Lois sleeping here, didn't we? Remember?
REID: Yes.
MOTHER: She was a good baby, wasn't she?
REID: We never waked her up.
MOTHER: Oh no. 'Cos you were so good as well.
REID: I just was going upstairs to bed and I never woke her up.

They return to the story and Reid's mother signals that they have nearly
reached the end:

MOTHER: Shall we just finish the end of the story, see if they all got what they
    wanted?

She sees an occasion for asking Reid to guess the correct words; this is
the only time in the story, apart from reading the title, when she has
drawn his attention to the actual text:

MOTHER: I want you to help me remember what they all wanted now. 'The
    mouse had ...'
REID: Cheese.
MOTHER: 'and the dog had a ...'

REID: ... Bone.
MOTHER: 'Jane had ...'
REID: Cake.

And so the story ends happily. Throughout Reid's mother has controlled the story-reading session by eliciting certain responses from Reid at various points in the story. She has a clear sense of what she wants him to do as they read together and uses particular strategies to achieve this. Reid, at the same time, is learning that a story-reading session involves knowing that a book has a title, listening to an adult reading, guessing some of the words himself when invited to do so, remembering how the story goes if it is one he has heard before, using events from his own life to match against the events of the story and discussing these. He knows it is perfectly valid for him to deviate from the text if this seems appropriate and expects to be listened to by the person reading the story. When Reid starts school he will probably have similar expectations about the way grown-ups there will share a book with him.

Here, eight weeks after starting school, he and I read *Where The Wild Things Are* together. He already knows the story well and wants to share and celebrate his previous knowledge with me. He likes the story and he knows that I like it. I invite him to tell me the title, just as his mother did, and together we set up a context for the reading time together:

REID: '*Where The Wild Things Are.*' Can you read it to me?
HM: You join in where you want to.

I begin to read, then Reid joins in and takes over the telling of the story:

HM: 'The night Max wore his wolf suit and made mischief of one kind – '
REID: And his room changes into a forest.

He's telling himself the story all over again. He remembers what Max says, then tells me what will happen to Max's bedroom carpet:

REID: 'I'm gonna eat you ...
HM: ' ... and another. His mother called him Wild Thing and Max said I'll eat you up, and so he was sent to bed without eating anything. That very night in Max's room a forest grew ...'
REID: I bet it's going to be part of the grass [pointing to Max's bedroom carpet].
HM: The carpet?
REID: I bet it's going to be the part of the grass.

HM: *It is!*
REID: *Yes, it is!*

Long before Reid came to school he had made the discovery that the
storyworld in the book stays the same across readings and across time,
and this knowledge enables him to hold this fictional world of Max's steady
in his head while sharing the book with me. Reid has always been invited
by his parents to respond to stories in ways which give him full par-
ticipatory rights in the interpretation of both text and illustrations, and
he continues to respond in this way at school. His previous readings of
this story have given him a memory for the narrative, and although he
knew that the carpet would become the grass (and probably knew that
I knew) he nevertheless needed to present the information to me as though
it was a surprise for both of us. I think he does this as a way of celebrating
his knowledge and memory. I carry on reading and Reid joins in when
he feels he wants to, confident and relaxed:

HM: ... 'a forest grew ... and grew' ...
REID: and grew ... till it ...
HM: 'till his ceiling hung with vines and the walls became the world all
   around' ...
REID: He founded a pirate a pirate boat for him.
HM: 'That night ...'
REID: And it says Max.
HM: Yes. 'And he sailed off through night and day ...'

No adult, at home or at school, has ever put Reid in the position of
feeling that he will not succeed as a reader. He has always been encouraged
to follow his inclination to make sense of what he reads. The messages
he is receiving are that reading is something for him: something he is entitled to as of right, and something that he can achieve easily. Three weeks
after coming to school he tells me about his books: 'I've got thousands
of books at home,' he says, 'in my bedroom, and in the library room.'

The attention paid to written language in his home has helped him
to begin to understand how language functions, and to identify himself
as a language user. He knows the meaning of 'word' when he tells me:
'I can't read really. Amber shows me how to read but I can't read this.
I can't really read. Amber showed me how I can read. How I can really
read so I can do the words.' His growing interest in the meaning of
language can be seen when he asks his teacher about a particular word

when he and Anthony, also four and a half, read *Mr Gumpy's Outing* with her:

ANTHONY: Can I go, said the sheep.
TEACHER: 'Yes, but don't keep *bleating.'*
ANTHONY: *bleating*
REID: What's bleeding mean?
TEACHER: That's the sound the sheep makes. When it goes baa-baa, we call that bleating.
REID: I thought you said bleeding.
TEACHER: No. Bleating.

As the story progresses Reid leaves his classroom behind as he enters the world of the story and demonstrates to his teacher, with Anthony's help, his ability to deal with narrative events:

TEACHER: ... 'and into the water they fell.'
ANTHONY: Splash!
REID: Splash went the boat.
ANTHONY: It was a big boat that was. He shouldn't let them in.
TEACHER: I hope they could all swim.
ANTHONY: I think so.
REID: The cat won't be able to.
TEACHER: Won't it?
REID: No.
ANTHONY: Cats can't swim.
TEACHER: Can't they? I don't think pigs can swim either.

This is the kind of conversation he has been used to at home when Reid shares a book with his parents and it seems to trigger a memory of canoeing, and perhaps of being a little afraid of the water:

TEACHER: Perhaps the water won't be too deep. Perhaps their feet will reach the bottom.
REID: The other day I went to a swimming baths and I had a seat in a canoe boat with me and I went in a massive ... I went in first the children's boat then the mummy and daddy's boat and there was a deep end and a little end.
TEACHER: A deep end and a shallow end was it?
REID: And we taked the boat into the other one then I ... I went on my own.
TEACHER: Did you?
REID: But I had to have someone with me. That was my Liam.
TEACHER: And he helped look after you. Make sure you were safe ... they needed somebody to look after them, didn't they, in the story?

Reid's teacher is an attentive and careful listener and helps both children to respond to the story by taking account of their comments and suggestions. She makes no attempt to make Reid learn individual words in the story, though she does attend to words by responding to his question about 'bleeding' and suggesting the use of 'shallow' in place of 'little'. But the story is there to be enjoyed and the teacher trusts that the children's interest in language will develop alongside their enjoyment of books.

One day, six months after starting school, Reid and Helen, also aged four and a half, read some Michael Rosen poems together from *You Can't Catch Me*. Reid's teacher has read a good many poems to the class this year, and the children know some of them well. Reid has always liked funny poems. Before he came to school he used to ask his father to read Spike Milligan's *Silly Verse For Kids*, and now at school Michael Rosen is a favourite with the class. The children know some of his poems by heart. Here, Reid and Helen sit together and decide which poem they will read; this act of choosing is itself a significant part of learning to read, because it involves a commitment on the part of the reader to the text:

REID: I'll have that one.
HELEN: [leafing through the pages] What about 'Jo-Jo'? ... I've had that one ... I don't know that one, do you?
REID: No.
HELEN: Do you know that one or that one?

Eventually they opt for 'Down Behind the Dustbin' and Reid begins to read aloud. Helen interrupts him, when he reads 'Jim' instead of 'Sid'. She knows the verse goes differently:

REID: 'Down behind the dustbin
I met a dog called Jim
He said he didn't know me –'
HELEN: Not Jim. Sid.

Reid isn't used to being corrected like this. Normally the adults who read with him accept his version of the story as long as it makes sense. Helen, though, has a memory of the rhyme and needs it to be correct. Reid asks for clarification:

REID: What? I can't hear what you're saying.

and Helen tells him the correct version:

HELEN: 'Down behind the dustbin
I met a dog called Sid
He said he didn't know me
But I said he surely did.'

Reid has now heard the rhyme read correctly and he has another go, but falters at the word 'Sid'. Helen tells him again, but perhaps her assertiveness and insistence on accuracy upset him. Certainly, his reading is now without rhythm:

REID: 'Down behind the dustbin
I met a dog called ... '
HELEN: Sid
REID: 'Sid. I said he ... he said he ... '
HELEN: 'He didn't know *me*'
REID: *me*
HELEN: 'But I said he – '
REID: '*surely did*'.
HELEN: '*surely did*'.

I think that if Helen were an adult I would consider her to be rather heavy-handed in her approach, but she is not an adult, and this rhyme to her mind has to be correct. The relationship between the two children is not the same as a relationship between an adult and a child, though in this case Reid has things he could learn from Helen.

Reid arrived at school with a deep understanding of narrative and now in the classroom he often makes up his own stories as he draws (Figure 10), creating his own imaginative world in his head and using it to reflect on his own life by shaping and giving some sort of meaning to his experience:

> One day this policeman saw naughty people being naughty. Then they went to get them. He's very sad 'cos he didn't want to go to jail 'cos he was sorry to be naughty. The policeman said to the little boy, 'You shouldn't have done that.' Because then the light was flashing. He switched the light on 'cos it was getting dark. Then before it was night time I had a biscuit and a drink. Then they lived happily ever after. And that's the end.

Events such as these have never actually happened to Reid, yet the feelings they generate – a sense of guilt at doing wrong, fear of retribution and finally the need for comfort and warmth – are there deep inside him and need to be explored in the safety of a story. He uses this story to

Figure 10

give him a way of examining and accepting blame and retribution for wrong done and finally making things all right again, through the symbolic comfort of food. This theme runs through that most important of books *Where The Wild Things Are*, which Reid knows and loves. It comes as no surprise, then, to find that a month later Reid is once again needing to explore these feelings in a story. He sat at his table and drew a car again (Figure 11) saying, 'This is a different story about that boy who gets lost, but there's going to be a different thing on it.' And he told this story as he drew:

One day the car when it was green the car just went and the people got run over by an ambulance. The ambulance stopped quickly because there was a car coming. Then they was pretending let's creep out. Now they went into

Figure 11

a shop where there was cakes and they smashed the window and they ate one without paying. Then the police came and got the money and took them to jail. Then you could say then the policeman took the cake out of them and put it back in the cake shop.

These two stories are about growing up, balancing that yearning for independence, with its accompanying fears of getting lost and going astray, against the need for the warmth and safety of the known. Reid is using narrative in these two stories to reshape and come to terms with events in his own life where he may have been naughty and felt guilt, and he matches this experience against the story of the people who have broken the law, with the policeman representing the authority figure. In other words Reid, as skilled narrator, has crafted these stories in a way which allows him to work out an ethical code for himself.

By the end of his second term in school Reid has taken twenty books home to read. Most are story books; one is an information book about making an indoor garden and one is a book of poems; he has followed his own inclination in his choices and expects each text to make sense to him, evidence of his confidence in himself as a reader. His awareness of his own needs as a language user suggests that he will become a successful reader and writer in the future.

PART TWO

Further Considerations

6

Learning to Read

It is time now to begin looking more closely at what these young children already know about reading. They are still inexperienced, of course, about many areas, but I believe that they already possess a wide range of abilities, some that mark them out as specialists in certain aspects of reading. They know a great deal about community uses of print, they use their narrative skills to help them read story books, and they are beginning to discover how language works. This early literacy learning is integral to their reading development and is supported by interaction with other people at home and in the wider community, with books, the media and the world of advertising. This learning can easily be overlooked or discounted, especially if we have not been taught to see it; if we have been told that the ability to recognise individual words in a book or to 'build words up' from the sounds their letters make are the first signs of reading success in the young child, we will not pay attention to the kinds of print young children have access to before they come to school and what significance it has for them.

But if we do allow ourselves to take a wider view of the whole process of becoming a reader, what do we see? Well, we see children already at ease with a great deal of the print they see around them: they know about it because it is part of the fabric of their lives before they come to school, interwoven in the daily transactions with family and community. Anthony instantly recognises *Weetabix* and *Cocopops* because they are his two favourite cereals; Gemma knows about tins of peas and beans; Reid sends for his free tennis balls from a *Start* packet. The media play their part too: Anthony knows the titles of television programmes and videos he watches: 'He-Man', 'She-Ra', 'Knight-Rider', *Jaws*, 'The A-Team', 'Airwolf'; Gurdeep is absorbed by Transformers and recognises the name on

television, on his advertising brochure and on his school lunchbox. Geeta
has learned about Care Bears. Collectively, the children's pre-school
knowledge of community print takes in the following areas: food labels,
newspapers, shopping catalogues, calendars (in English and Punjabi), advertisements (in brochures, catalogues and on television), birthday cards, wedding and party invitations (in English and Punjabi), letters, bills, crosswords,
the writing on coins and bank notes, pools coupons, lists, diet sheets,
tickets, appointment cards, number plates and maps. And though most
books follow the conventional left-to-right sequencing of the English
language, and children have to know this, it's worth noting that many
forms of print that they are in daily contact with do not follow a simple
left-to-right convention and may even present words in a totally different
format. Gurdeep is fascinated by coins, which require him to read round
the edge in a circular fashion, and by bank notes, with their many different writing layouts. The children frequently read lists (top to bottom
as well as left to right) and see newspapers set out in columns, with
headlines. Gemma watches her father do the crossword, and sees him
write words from top to bottom as well as left to right. And the children
may meet the word 'Ambulance' written not only right to left but with
the letters laterally inverted, so they can be read in a car driver's mirror:

ƎƆИA⅃U8MA

These are complex reading lessons indeed!

In addition to this vast store of knowledge, the children have begun
to learn about how to read a book long before they learn to pay attention to the actual print. Reid, for instance, knows how to use an illustration from *Where The Wild Things Are* to help him make sense of the
story: 'I bet that's going to be part of the grass' (p. 69). Geeta learns about
authorship as she reads *The Snowman* – 'He wrote *The Snowman*? All
of this?' (p. 55). Gurdeep retells the story of *Where The Wild Things Are*
in his own words: 'Then he's going to kill the dog. Dog ... ranned ...
he runned away' (p. 16). Gemma uses literary language to retell *Goldilocks
and the Three Bears*: 'Porridge was too hot and they set off out in the
woods. Long time ago' (p. 26). And Anthony learns to be a critical reader

as he shares *Mr Gumpy's Outing* with his teacher: 'It was a big boat that was. He shouldn't have let them in' (p. 71).

Strategies like these help young children to make their way through a book, often with help, unravelling the meaning as they go along and demonstrating such a strong desire to read, to understand what is on the page, that I marvel at their intelligent commitment. The rest of this chapter will be concerned with the children's response to books, highlighting some of the ways they are beginning to learn.

Each time these young readers are presented with a poem or a story, they have to come to grips with its meaning. This involves them in a process of making connections between the story and their own lives, and they do this most frequently through talk. Reid, for example, helped by an attentive teacher and his experience of reading with his parents, forges a link between his own boat story and the occasion when Mr Gumpy's boat sank (p. 71):

REID: The other day I went to a swimming baths and I had a seat in a canoe boat with me and I went in a massive ... I went in first the children's boat then the mummy and daddy's boat and there was a deep end and a little end.
TEACHER: A deep end and a shallow end was it?
REID: And we taked the boat into the other one then I ... I went on my own.
TEACHER: Did you?
REID: But I had to have someone with me. That was my Liam.
TEACHER: And he helped look after you. Make sure you were safe ... they needed somebody to look after them, didn't they, in the story?

By listening carefully Reid's teacher supports him as he reformulates the story of *Mr Gumpy's Outing* in terms of his previous experience of boats and water, and perhaps of being frightened of falling in. This helps him to understand a little more deeply how the characters feel when they are in Mr Gumpy's boat and almost certainly gives Reid the same kind of satisfaction as adults get when they read demanding literature.

Reading involves children in a search for meaning, for understanding. In order to know a story, to get into the heads of the characters, to put themselves into the scene, to fantasise, children have to be given opportunities by parents and teachers to respond as Reid does here, and as Gemma does when her mother reads with her (p. 23):

MOTHER: 'The raindrops make lots of little – '
GEMMA: And the man and that says I am under an umbrella. When the rain stops the umbrella goes on that man.

MOTHER: Yeah, that's right. Covers him 'cos of the rain.
GEMMA: Like you, Mum.
MOTHER: Yes.

Gemma takes over the reading in a way that pleases and satisfies her: note too how much she already knows about using literary language as she shares this story with her mother – 'when the rain stops the umbrella goes on that man' – this is different from the kind of language she uses in normal conversations. She has understood, unconsciously, that the language used in books is a special kind of language, not normally used in everyday conversation, and it has its own structure and rhythm. A good example of this 'book language' is the version of *Little Red Riding Hood* which Anthony's mother reads to him.

> 'Little Red Riding Hood's father took her by the hand and led her thankfully back to her mother, and how happy she was that things had turned out so well. "As long as I live," said Little Red Riding Hood, "I shall never leave the forest path when you have warned me not to do so." ' (p. 82)

She would never speak to Anthony in everyday conversation using this kind of language, but as he listens to her he begins to try out this kind of language for himself, using a 'book voice', as he retells *Little Red Riding Hood* in his own words, using phrases closer to written than spoken language:[1]

> Once upon a time there was Little Red Riding Hood. She went into the woods and she met a big bad wolf. And he hurried on to the woods. He got there just in time. He pulled the latch and came in. He ate Grandmother in one mouthful. (p. 40)

Anthony's mother did not consciously teach him to use this new form of language; nevertheless he met it frequently when he began listening to her read to him before he started school, taking on the role Cochran-Smith calls 'reader-as-spokesperson-for-text'.[2] In other words his mother is no longer talking to him, as she would in everyday conversation: she is reading aloud using someone else's words. This is something quite different, and Anthony knows his mother's speaking voice has changed when she reads: 'I shall never leave the forest path when you have warned me not to do so'.[3] Gurdeep also uses the patterns and rhythms of the prose of the original book with confidence as he retells *Where The Wild Things Are*, using words and phrases he remembers:

They gnashed their terrible ... gnashed they gnashed their terrible ... ter ... eyes. Tashed their terrible. Tashed their terrible teeth and ... (p. 16)

Gurdeep struggles on. He knows the words of the story cannot change and, driven by a need to get them right, to make them sound the way he knows the book goes, he practises over and over again, all the time getting closer to the actual language of the book:

Tashed their terrible teeth and tashed their terr – showed their terrible claws.

Gurdeep is not unusual in spending time retelling stories like this; I hear Gemma, Anthony, Geeta and Reid sharing stories with their friends or with an adult in a similar fashion, using their own words and at the same time echoing the original book language. Children learn to control the pace of their own reading by retelling stories; they can choose to vary the speed, to pause, or to go back over a part – to learn, in other words, to become autonomous readers. Perhaps this goes some way towards explaining their powerful need to retell a story and make it their own, turning the printed version into something familiar. The urge to tell a story is strong, almost unstoppable.

Children are good narrators before they come to school, and by encouraging them to tell the story off the page we not only give them an opportunity to do what comes easily to them, we also allow them to experience what it feels like to get through an entire book, to complete the whole task, even though they know very little as yet about recognising individual words in the story or 'building up' words from their letter-sounds. Children come to know what reading entails by doing it for themselves and experiencing success in this way. They know what it is they have to do and they know where their learning is leading; thus they provide good reading models for themselves and for each other.[4]

As I listen to the children sharing stories with each other or with an adult I notice that they are often doing something quite sophisticated in their reading, as this brief extract from Gurdeep's retelling of *Where The Wild Things Are* shows:

GURDEEP: ' ... mother said no ... ah ... no I missed the other page ... Ah he said mother ... '

The comment (p. 16), almost delivered as an aside, shows Gurdeep operating within the story and then just as easily taking himself out of that make-believe world and back to reality to account for a break in the telling.

(As he becomes more experienced, and learns to read silently, I suspect that he will not be troubled by this kind of break because he will concentrate wholly on the meaning; but this reading is aloud and Simon is his audience. This makes Gurdeep's retelling into a kind of performance and he needs to verbalise what he's done, both for himself and for Simon.) His comment shows that he is learning about the nature of books and the relationship between the books as an artefact and the reality of his minute-by-minute existence. It is the beginning of his discovery of narrative time and real time; a discovery, therefore, about symbolism and metaphor. The world of the book always stays the same but his life constantly moves forward and Gurdeep takes himself in and out of both worlds with ease.

Gurdeep's comment is unprovoked; Anthony is helped to formulate what he wants to say by a more experienced reader, in this case his teacher, who helps him to place himself at a distance from the events of the book in a most sophisticated way.[5] Although he is clearly absorbed and fascinated by the story of *Mr Gumpy's Outing*, Anthony is able to detach himself from the events in order to evaluate Mr Gumpy's actions, because he is not actually involved in them himself.[6] His response is the beginning of a critical response to fiction:

TEACHER: 'and into the water they fell.'
ANTHONY: Splash!
REID: Splash went the boat.
ANTHONY: It was a big boat that was. He shouldn't have let them in.
TEACHER: I hope they could all swim. (p. 71)

'Spectating' on people and possibilities in this way may appear to be rather a mature process to have observed in the reading behaviour of such young children; nevertheless, it is there and they use it, as they use so much of their early knowledge, to help them make sense of the books themselves and, perhaps more importantly, of their own lives.[7]

I notice too that the children are learning about such things as knowing what a title is, where to open a book up, finding where the story begins and where to turn the page. They are also mastering such physical operations as holding the book and co-ordinating hand and eye movements so that text and illustrations are visible. Children who have their books held for them and their pages turned for them may be slower to learn this handling process. Children also have to learn to direct their gaze from left to right and around the page to make the text and illustrations work together to help the story unfold – good writers, illustrators and editors work to make this task easier – though of course there are many kinds of print which have to be read quite differently (see above, p. 80). And most importantly, children also have to learn which parts of the book they need not read.[8]

Gurdeep, Geeta, Gemma, Reid and Anthony have already been helped by parents or nursery teachers to learn many of these skills [9] and it is more than likely that the teaching they received was implicit and indirect.[10] I remember my own mother would put me on her knee for my afternoon sleep while holding her book in her free hand, deftly turning each page by crooking her little finger under the page and levering it over. She never talked to me about this but I watched her with fascination and later taught myself how to do it. Anthony needs to know how to match his knowledge of how a story goes (he knows it has a beginning, a middle and an end) to the conventions of the book's layout (p. 42). Here he asks his teacher some important questions:

ANTHONY: Is this the beginning?
TEACHER: No. That tells us the title, look *Mr Gumpy's Outing*. And that's the name of the man who wrote it. John Burningham.
ANTHONY: Is that the end? [pointing to the next blank page]
TEACHER: No. We have to turn over to find the beginning.

Anthony's questions show that he knows about the structure of a story – that it has a beginning and an end – but he isn't sure how to relate this knowledge to the format of the book. As his teacher helps him, she also tells him what a title is and about people who write books. Part of learning how a book works is learning the concept of authorship – that books are written by real people, and illustrated by real people.

Geeta needs to know more about this too (p. 59):

TEACHER: *The Noisiest Class in School*. By Pauline Hill.
GEETA: Pauline Hill.
TEACHER: That's Pauline Hill wrote the words in the book, wrote the story.
GEETA: All the pictures?
TEACHER: No. The pictures, the illustrations, were by Joan Beales.
GEETA: Joan Beales.
TEACHER: That's another lady.
GEETA: That's another lady.

TEACHER: It is, yes.
GEETA: Who drew the pictures?
TEACHER: Joan Beales.
GEETA: Joan Beales.
TEACHER: That's right. Go on then. You turn the page over.

She needs to know about titles too (p. 55):

GEETA: What's that say? [pointing to the title]
HM: 'The Snowman.'
GEETA: The Snowman. That's all said Snowman? [pointing to the title again]

In this way Geeta demonstrates how she is coming to terms with this new learning.

As children become more skilled language users their interest in graphic information grows and they begin to make discoveries about the structures and functions of written language. They are interested in print, especially when it has a bearing on their lives – food labels, toys, advertisements, birthday cards, and so on, and their comments and questions show that they are beginning to attend to language itself as they find ways of talking about it in order to make their meaning explicit.[11] There are several instances where the children talk about language:

GEETA: You've got two of these in your name [pointing to letter e].
ANTHONY: Have I got an A in my name?
GEMMA: ..., and that says 'Daddy'.
REID: I'm good at writing.
GEETA: When I'm big I'll write a hard story and a sentence.
GEMMA: Does that say my name?

The children are beginning to use specialised vocabulary – like 'sentence', 'word' and 'writing'; they are making reference to letters and beginning to learn that names are composed of letters.[12]

The process of knowing how to recognise and represent their own name in writing seems to be a crucial part of learning what language is about. The children are all deeply interested in the fact that their own names can be represented on paper, that it is a permanent marker even though they may go away from where it was written (Gemma's name remains on her birthday cards even when she puts them away and closes the drawer). This learning is very powerful. It is as though by seeing themselves represented in print, and learning to write their name, children are able to develop a new awareness about what language is and what it can be used for.

It is at this time too that children begin to exploit their new knowledge of language to play with it and to have fun with it, and they use it to make rhymes and jokes. These have a social function too, and Anthony enjoys teasing his mother at the same time as he is learning about the rules and meaning of language (p. 37):

ANTHONY: Mum, do you want me to tell you a joke about the butter?
MUM: What is it?
ANTHONY: You can't spread it 'cos it might melt.

Anthony hasn't quite got it right; the real joke goes something like this:

– Do you know the one about the butter?
– Go on, tell me.
– No. It's a secret. You might spread it.

He probably knows both meanings of 'spread' but like a lot of young children, he isn't yet able to make the simultaneous comparison which the telling of this joke requires. He is, though, busy learning a complex linguistic process. All the humour of this joke is contained in the language itself; there's no support from a comic strip or a television image, and Anthony has to work hard to put the total meaning across to his mother.[13]

Adult experienced readers can build on children's discoveries about written language by responding to their individual needs: by listening to and joining in with their jokes, as Anthony's mother does; by helping to find a name on a birthday card, as Gemma's mother does; or by helping a child to find more letter 'e's' on a page, as Geeta's teacher does (p. 60):

GEETA: Looks like my name up there [pointing to 'Gene'].
TEACHER: Yes. Your name begins with that letter.
GEETA: Yes. You've got two of those in your name [pointing to the 'e' in 'Gene'].
TEACHER: Yes. A 'G' and two 'e's'. Gene's got a 'G' and two 'e's' in his name.

These adult responses take Gemma, Geeta and Anthony forward from the point they have reached in a way that is compatible with their whole literacy learning.

All five children are beginning to develop positive views about themselves as readers, and are developing a feel for reading. This gives them the confidence to expect that they will be able to understand what a book or poem is about and to take risks with their reading. They are able to recognise some of the words and memorise some lines of the text; they have a sense of literary language; they are learning to use language to talk about language; they are learning about the conventions of a book; in fact, their early reading competencies mean that they do a great many things experienced readers do. Throughout the time I observed them they have used all their cognitive and emotional resources to help them make sense of what is there in front of them on the page.

Many of the examples I have used in this chapter come from the children's readings of story books; this is no coincidence. Stories – those they invent for themselves and those they discover in books – are crucially important to children, and it is to the world of the story that we turn our attention in the next chapter.

7

Entering Fairyland: A Child's Sense of Story

In the last chapter I looked at what the children already know about learning to read, paying particular attention to the strategies they use as they learn to read story books. This chapter extends that discussion by exploring in more detail the importance of story and literature in their lives and in the process of learning to read – stories they invent for themselves in their play, stories they tell themselves about their own lives, stories they hear from those around them and stories they meet in books.

When we enter a world made purely by the imagination, our own or that of others, we elect to leave behind our normal everyday existence and instead invest our lives with a new set of circumstances and possibilities that allow us to consider for ourselves different pasts and possible futures. We extend our experience vicariously as we dream, daydream, read and tell each other stories about ourselves and others; and if we are young children, we use narrative form in our pre-sleep monologues [1] and we also play. [2]

When children play – on their own or together – they step outside their own lives and enter a world of their imaginings. This is a creative process involving enormous energy, intelligence, self-discipline and single-mindedness, as Anthony and Mark's Lego game shows (p. 40):

ANTHONY: Mine can change into something else. These couldn't fight us 'cos they were goodies and they could fly.
MARK: They have to go up, don't they?
ANTHONY: [takes wheels] Pretend these batter us ... mine's bashed up.
MARK: Mine still ain't broken.
ANTHONY: I'm coming to transform you.

The boys use Lego to create a twenty-minute-long Transformer fantasy for themselves. There's enormous excitement and commitment as they release themselves from the powerlessness of childhood into a world where they are fully in control of situations and their own destinies:

MARK: I'm dead now [he throws Lego on the floor].
ANTHONY: You don't fall 'cos I go faster. You can't still kill me.
MARK: This is your last chance. The wheels killed me once but they can't kill me twice.

Geeta and Sherine, in the house corner, use their imaginative play to help them take control of their world and possible futures (p. 53).

SHERINE: Come on, Mum.
GEETA: I'm not Mum. We're two sisters.
SHERINE: You hold the dog. I'll have the baby [she gets a doll out of the box for herself and a toy dog for Geeta].
GEETA: We both have babies [she reaches in the box for another doll]. This is my baby and I'll have the dog too. I'm going to the park.

This rehearsal for adulthood and family life helps Geeta and Sherine to learn about the world around them, their families and their place within the family structure. They act out the role of mother and sister and in so doing, take control of themselves and their world.

Anthony and Mark, and Sherine and Geeta, use props like Lego, dolls, a toy dog, and so on, alongside their talk to help them invent and act out their stories, but they don't necessarily need toys to help them do this. Gurdeep, Anthony and Reid show that they are equally skilled in creating a world through their talk which they 'act out' on paper, drawing the action as they tell the story. Gurdeep draws his imaginary world as he shapes a story with his language:

> One day there was a robot. His name was Optimus Prime and he was the Transformers' leader. All the baddy evils came to fight and Optimus Prime quickly changed. Then the fight was finished and the baddy ones were all burned. More baddy evils came and quickly changed again and they fought and Optimus Prime won again.

Gurdeep is a skilled storyteller. The stories he has met at home and the cartoons and television programmes he watches (including the advertisements, which increasingly seem to tell a story) have helped him to shape a story in the past tense with a beginning and an ending. Anthony structures the events of a story too, though his narrative is ongoing and he doesn't have a clear beginning and ending:

> That's me. Well, I've been doing a lot of fishing. I went fishing. A shark came up and it bit me right here where it's all swollen. My dad put a bomb in its mouth and it blowed all to pieces. Going to put a bomb in his mouth and it blowed up. All the tooth came up one by one and I picked them up and I threw the teeth away in the bin and all the blood came up. And I seen the belly come up. (p. 45)

Reid knows all about the literary conventions of storytelling and he weaves an intricate tale, with the expectation of judgement for wrongdoing intertwined with the sense of a happy ending:

> One day this policeman saw naughty people being naughty. Then they went to get them. He's very sad 'cos he didn't want to go to jail 'cos he was sorry to be naughty. The policeman said to the little boy, 'You shouldn't have done that.' Because then the light was flashing. He switched the light on 'cos it was getting dark. Then before it was night time I had a biscuit and a drink. Then they lived happily ever after. And that's the end. (p. 73)

There's the same power and energy and creative force at work here to sustain the telling of these tales as we saw in the playhouse game and the Lego game.

Our lives are made up of stories and children quickly learn to create a sense of order in their own lives by telling stories about themselves, thus giving themselves a history and an identity. Gurdeep creates the story of his life when he views photographs in his album and takes control of his past by telling this story:

> When I was in hospital I was a baby ... there's my mum holding me ... I had a needle in my arm and then I went out ... I'm coming out of hospital ... now I'm going home ... this is my grandma and mum and my auntie holding me ... now I'm grown up. (p. 9)

Gurdeep tells this story by remembering events as they have been told to him. He creates memories for himself as he links these events into a narrative and in this way gives himself an identity, a unique place in the world. One day his story may change when he feels the need to insert other events and experiences into his past and perhaps omit others that are no longer significant for him. And he may choose to relate different histories to different people, depending on circumstances. It is our ability to shape our lives in this way that anchors us and gives us a view of ourselves as we are now, as we were as children, and as we may be in the future. Geeta plans a future identity for herself as a writer when she remarks: 'When I'm big I'll write a hard story.'

It is one small step to introduce the notion of the story book into the children's already familiar world of play and storytelling. The kind of book we choose to put into these children's hands is crucial and we need to exercise great care and skill in what we select for them to read. These young children are skilled storytellers and we have a responsibility to give them stories that validate those they tell themselves. We know from their play and their own oral stories that they can handle important themes like conflict, death, looking after babies, suspense, punishment, family relationships, their pasts and their futures, and are able to deal with these powerful ideas and experiences in their own rich literary language. The story books we offer them need to reflect this complexity so children can use them to enter the imaginary world inside the cover and explore new situations and experiences, just as they do in the house corner, or with the Lego or on paper, or through their photographs.

As the five children's reading lives unfold we see them reading and sharing different kinds of story and literature: European fairy tales, Indian moral tales, modern picture-story books, poems, and of course their own dictated stories transcribed and made up into books. When a child opens up a book, he or she finds that the author has already set the scene: perhaps it's Max's bedroom [3] or the river by Mr Gumpy's house, or a deep dark forest. The child enters each world, using the book as a toy or a prop, 'playing' with it and creating a story from its pages; for this is what he or she has to do. Without that act of creation on their part, there can be no story.

The best stories offer children a chance to explore, in symbolic form, the problems and possibilities involved in being born, in growing up and dying: the challenges, struggles and physical dangers of existing in the human world resound through the pages of these books. These are big themes, forming the substance of folk-fairy tales, myths and legends of many cultures, [4] and may appear in the guise of giants, wolves, witches, bears, monsters, or as quests to be undertaken. They are the stuff of fables, too – the tortoise story that Gurdeep's mother tells is a lesson in how life should be lived within a particular cultural tradition (p. 11).

The conflicts and tensions of growing towards independence and maturity are examined equally powerfully in modern picture-story books, where danger appears in the shape of a fox in *Rosie's Walk* and anger takes on the form of a Wild Thing in *Where The Wild Things Are*. The themes are the same: the need to go out into the world is set against the fear of losing the security of the home; the rage against powerlessness is tempered by the responsibilities of power; fear of dying is countered by the need to love and to be loveable. It is little wonder that some children need to reread a particular story many times because it contains meanings which they need to hold on to – Anthony's need for *Little Red Riding Hood* is a good example of this (p. 40). Authors of good children's books are deeply aware of what children need to read about and present their stories in a form children can understand and respond to. Writers like Maurice Sendak, John Burningham, Pat Hutchins, Shirley Hughes, Raymond Briggs, David McKee, and many more are able to present deep universal experiences and emotions in ways children can handle in safety, between the covers of a book.

We should not be surprised that many of these stories have overlapping themes and that children become skilled in carrying meaning from one book to another as they learn more about individual stories and about how stories work. Some modern children's writers deliberately exploit children's knowledge and skill by introducing into their stories characters and events that come straight out of traditional tales, relying on children's knowledge of other stories to make the new story work. Geeta shows how she does this when she and I share *The Jolly Postman* together. In this book different characters from fairy tales receive letters written to them by characters in their own story. One illustration shows the three bears receiving a letter from Goldilocks and Geeta immediately recognises the three bears as the same three bears she knows already from the fairy tale:

GEETA: Three bears. One daddy one, one mummy one, one baby one. We got three bears of that, haven't we? (p. 56)

It is significant that Geeta is looking closely at the illustration as she recognises the three bears. Illustrations in good children's picture-story books enrich and extend the text in this way to make a book work for children. Not only do they help children to recognise characters and see what they are doing but also, because they lead their eyes and minds forward, they enable children to get through a book by turning from one

picture to the next, one sentence to the next, and one page to the next.
Children are often able to anticipate events because illustrations carry subtle
clues about the nature of the story that go unmentioned in the text –
for instance, there is a drawing of a Wild Thing at the bottom of Max's
staircase in *Where The Wild Things Are*, but it is never referred to directly. And Reid's comment on the same book is revealing: 'I bet it's going
to be part of the grass' (p. 69), he says, as he points to Max's carpet
and waits for Max's bedroom to begin growing into a forest. Children
who watch films and videos learn to interrogate the moving picture in
much the same way and know how to 'read' subtle clues in the form
of images on the screen. Children interrogate illustrations in picture books
closely and respond to them, often through their talk, when they share
a book with another child or with an adult experienced reader. This gives
the child the feeeling of creating a story alongside the author; good writers
of children's stories don't tell them everything about the story. They require them to shape it for themselves and to be concerned about the
characters. [5] For example, we are never told directly in *Where The Wild
Things Are* that Max is sailing away from his mother, yet Gurdeep and
many other children know intuitively what Max is up to:

HM: Who is he sailing away from?
GURDEEP: From his mother.
HM: Why?
GURDEEP: 'Cos he's very naughty boy.
HM: Why does he want to go away?
GURDEEP: 'Cos he doesn't like her. (p. 13)

When children are exploring a world of their imagination, away from
the day-to-day world, they are doing something so clever, yet so subtle,
that we often miss its significance. Gurdeep's ability to leave behind the
real, immediate situation of the classroom table where we are sitting
reading, and enter voluntarily into a world of ideas as he follows Max's
journey, is a means for him to develop abstract thought processes. Gordon Wells recently undertook a major piece of research in which he
highlighted the importance of story in developing abstract thinking. [6]
Part of his evidence led him to believe that stories have a role in education that goes far beyond their contribution to the teaching of reading,
writing and literature because in order to understand a story a child has
to pay careful attention to the language alone in order to understand the

meaning. *This calls for higher levels of cognitive thinking*. The results of his research, he says, are unequivocal: the act of listening to stories at home is significantly associated with later success at school because high levels of cognitive thinking are necessary for learning.

Gurdeep makes this profound leap from his everyday surroundings into the world of the story as he enters an imaginary world made solely through the language of a book. He is working at the high cognitive level suggested by Wells because in order to make sense of the story he has to interpret the author's language and give it a meaning.[7] Anthony is operating at the same high cognitive level when he tells his mother the joke about the butter (p. 37). The humour of the joke is contained solely in the language. Similarly, when Anthony's teacher reads *The Elephant and the Bad Baby* to the class Anthony cannot look around the classroom for any clues about the meaning of this story – there are no elephants or babies to help him make sense of it. He has to be able to reconstruct Elvira Vipont's story for himself, using his own knowledge of elephants and babies and what it means to be 'bad'. We know he can do it successfully because his own retelling of the story goes like this:

> Once there was an elephant. Once there was a little bad baby. He said do you want a ride and the bad baby said yes. Went rumpeta, rumpeta, rumpeta all the way down the road. (p. 44)

Learning to read stories can never be a step-by-step matter of learning individual skills, perhaps by reading a page of the book each day or being encouraged to recognise a certain number of words each week. The process is far more complex than that, because the child is dealing in meanings which resonate through every aspect of their lives. Young children need to be given opportunities to talk their way through the story so that they can make connections between different stories, respond to characters and events, and find ways of linking the meaning of the story with meanings in their own lives, at a high intellectual level. In order to do this a child needs to read collaboratively with others who will help them towards that understanding and respond to the meanings they are making. The nature of this important relationship will be explored more fully in the next chapter.

8

Reading Partnerships

The reading biographies have shown that the children spend a great deal of their reading time in partnership with a skilled reader – a parent or teacher. These reading times, where the children learn and share a book with someone more experienced and skilled than themselves, illustrate the way in which the adult experienced reader fosters and maintains a successful reading partnership with the child learner.[1]

Every reading encounter in this study is, of course, unique because people bring their own personalities, cultural knowledge and interests to the task and take from the experience their own particular thoughts and satisfactions; and if there is a close personal relationship between adult and child they are almost bound to communicate in ways which go beyond the information in the story book. Taken as a whole, however, many of the story-reading sessions documented here share important features which show them to be particularly supportive to these young children who are in the early stages of becoming readers.[2]

I have in mind especially those story-reading times where the adult experienced reader takes responsibility for ensuring that the child's enjoyment and understanding of the story book are the central purpose of the reading. The adult initially takes control by setting up the situation for the reading to happen in the first instance and then takes overall responsibility for reading all or most of the story, frequently encouraging the child to respond through conversation.[3] The adult reader needs to be sensitive and flexible enough to read with a child in this way, and it is of note that so many of the adult experienced readers in this study approach the task with warmth, confidence and intelligence. Most notably, perhaps, *they make no outward distinction between reading and learning to read*, and thus put no pressure on the child to become 'word perfect' or to learn to recognise particular letter-sounds. Their aim, whether stated explicitly or not, is to involve the child as much as possible in understanding the author's words. They recognise that the child needs to talk about the story and give them time to do this. So the words of the story become intertwined with conversational talk; there are regular pauses to laugh at the funny bits, to enjoy repetitions aloud and to talk about things the story reminds them of. It is as if the adult knows, perhaps implicitly, that talking about incidents in a story, and matching them to things that have happened in real life, helps a child to understand the story at a deeper and more sophisticated level – as a critic of characters and situations in books and, by implication, of their own lives and actions.

There can obviously be no set formula for this kind of encounter between a skilled reader, a child and a book, but in these early stages of learning to read successful reading partnerships are likely to be those which are patterned in the way I have outlined, closely controlled by an adult experienced reader who sets up and maintains the conditions for learning and then trusts the child to learn. The adult knows too that the child learner has a particular role to play in this kind of reading partnership, since they are being asked to bring their own understanding to a book, actively, by working at the meaning. And there is a third person – the author, who, while not physically present at the story-book reading, is nevertheless represented through the words of the story, with the adult reader as mouthpiece. One of the tasks of the adult reader is to take responsibility for introducing the child and the author to each other.[4] Authors become the sleeping partners in the reading encounter and have a subtle part to play in the child's reading experience through the impact of their books and the way in which they are designed to be read and shared.[5]

The adult reader sets up the conditions for different kinds of reading to happen in a variety of ways: it might be when the family is out shopping (Reid's mother sets aside a special time when she can be on her own with him, helping him choose particular kinds of food for the family) or it could be on the settee at school (Geeta's teacher asks her to sit comfortably by her side as they share a book together) or perhaps in bed at home (where Gurdeep's father reads him a bedtime story). In all these examples it is the adult who encourages the child into a position of wanting to read, even though the task may be difficult and demanding, because it holds its own rewards: time alone with a caring adult; the fascination of a good story; the security that the bedtime story brings, tucked up warm between the sheets; the promise of food.

I do not want to suggest that the child has no part to play in negotiating reading time together (Reid often asks his teacher to read with him; and remember Gemma, who took a book into her home and pleaded with her mother to 'Read it to me now!'). Even so, in these cases it is still the adult who facilitates reading by allowing the child the freedom to ask, to initiate, perhaps by establishing a democratic classroom community or by including the child in decision-making about the use of time in the home, or out shopping. The adult is the principal organiser of time and space, whether at home or at school, and has the prime responsibility for initiating reading; this includes managing an environment where a child feels free to ask to read.

The adult reader, now sitting alongside the child, book in hand, has to decide how the book should be tackled. Who will read the book and who will be the listener? Or should the task be shared? How should the pictures be 'read' and understood as part of the story? How to begin – and how to finish? In successful reading partnerships the adult often talks with the child about how they will read through the book together and then gives the child as much information as they feel they can handle: in the early stages of reading this often involves telling the child the title of the book, or asking if they remember it. It's a way of setting the scene for what is to follow.

Reid's mother has read this book to him before and wonders if he will remember what it's called (p. 66):

MOTHER: Do you know what this book's called?

REID: Yes, the cat got stuck in ...

MOTHER: *That Fat Cat* it's called. So you were nearly right, weren't you? 'Once upon a time there was ...'

At school Reid and I share *Where The Wild Things Are*. I also begin by inviting him to tell me the title, just as his mother did (p. 69):

HM: Do you remember what it's called?

REID: *Where The Wild Things Are.*

Reid is used to decision-making at home, to being included in negotiations, and he is prepared to ask me for what he wants:

REID: Can you read it to me?

I nod that I will but want to give him the opportunity to take over parts of the reading if he wishes, so I say:

HM: You join in where you want to.

It is very important to involve Reid in these negotiations about how a book should be read, because in this way he is being kept at the centre of his own learning and thinking processes, made fully conscious of what he feels able to do alone and what he has to do in order to get the support he wants from a skilled reader.

   Geeta's teacher elects to introduce the book they are sharing by reading out the title and the name of the author (p. 59):

TEACHER: *The Noisiest Class in School.* By Pauline Hill.
GEETA: Pauline Hill.

It is significant that Geeta comes in immediately with a query about the author. Her teacher has made Geeta feel comfortable enough to ask about things that puzzle her by giving her equal rights to speak and ask questions and by being a good listener. She now has to decide how to explain the concept of authorship to the four-year-old:

TEACHER: That's Pauline Hill wrote the words in the book, wrote the story.

Geeta seems to need to know if 'story' means the pictures as well, and frames a question to help her understand:

GEETA: All the pictures?
TEACHER: No. The pictures, the illustrations, were by Joan Beales.
GEETA: Joan Beales.
TEACHER: That's another lady.
GEETA: That's another lady.
TEACHER: It is, yes.
GEETA: Who drew the pictures?
TEACHER: Joan Beales.
GEETA: Joan Beales.

There would have been no room for Geeta's preoccupation with these matters if her teacher had set up the reading situation differently, perhaps by expecting her to listen silently as she read the story. When she is satisfied that Geeta has understood she decides it is time to continue, handing the next task to Geeta:

TEACHER: That's right. Go on then. You turn the next page over.

Geeta's teacher knows her learner well and is able to build on the reading knowledge she has already. Notice that she does not turn the page for her; because Geeta is knowledgeable about handling a book, she is able to do this for herself. This also gives her the right to turn the page at her own speed, looking first at whatever interests her on the new page. Geeta's own role in all this is crucial: she knows it's her job to get meaning from the book with the support of her teacher by making comments, asking questions, and by her skill in handling the book. Her teacher helps her by giving her an explanation for things she doesn't understand. These learning conditions also enable Geeta to ask about new vocabulary. Normally, her teacher would not attempt to teach the meaning of an individual word in isolation but now Geeta is concerned to know the meaning of 'tatty', which she meets in the story. Her teacher helps her to put 'tatty' into a context which Geeta can understand (p. 59):

GEETA: What does tatty mean?
TEACHER: Tatty? Untidy. Not very nice.
GEETA: Not very nice?
TEACHER: A bit ripped, might be, tatty. Or a bit creased.
GEETA: Like this? [looking at her own blouse]
TEACHER: A bit creased like that, yes. But that isn't really tatty. That's creased because you've been wearing it all day.

Geeta's teacher knows that a story will rarely make sense to Geeta if she simply reads it to her, so she makes sure that all their reading times together include conversations like this. Her response depends on what Geeta has noticed in the story or the illustrations, what she has understood or was confused by, and how she interprets the story in terms of her own life. This way of setting up and maintaining a story-reading session allows Geeta to trust her teacher by asking her questions, and to become a conversational partner.

Gemma and her mother read together in much the same way: her mother reads from the book and then sets up a dialogue for Gemma to respond to (p. 23):

MOTHER: 'I take water from the dirty puddles and put it in the clean puddles. Now I have two dirty puddles.' Uggh! Isn't it dirty?
GEMMA: Uggh!

Gemma responds and her mother continues reading, but Gemma breaks into her reading to comment on an illustration and take over the reading for herself:

MOTHER: 'The raindrops make lots of little – '
GEMMA: And the man and that says I am under an umbrella. When the rain stops the umbrella goes on that man.
MOTHER: Yeah, that's right. Covers him 'cos of the rain.
GEMMA: Like you, Mum.
MOTHER: Yeah.

Gemma is finding her own way of making sense of this story by commenting on the situation and relating it to her own life – 'like you, Mum'. Her mother, implicitly, helps Gemma to construct the meaning of this episode by allowing her to use her own experience to reflect on new ideas, so that the story weaves in and out of Gemma's own personal life.

Geeta's teacher listens as Geeta begins a similar conversation, matching an event in a story to her own life and thus giving her a deeper understanding of what the author is saying (p. 60):

TEACHER: 'Our school has got a bus. It picks us all up each morning and takes us to school.'
GEETA: My dad goes to the factory and my mum and she come back to fetch me and goes back to the factory to eat her dinner.

Geeta's teacher could have led her back to the book at this point, but she decides to continue the conversation because she knows that it matters. Geeta does not arrive at school on a bus and the story gives her a way of framing her own day by reflecting on the way she is brought and collected and, by extension, telling the story of her mother's day and of the broken coffee machine:

TEACHER: She has her dinner at the factory?
GEETA: No, she brings her dinner at the factory 'cos we haven't got the coffee. We still haven't got any coffee, right. We got the machine of it so we got a new one. We got an old one, it's broken. It doesn't work for six months.

As Geeta examines her own life she develops a deeper understanding of the learning process itself, discovering that she is free to move away from the story if she wishes and that the meaning she brings to the story is valid.

Anthony and Reid are also learning about learning as they share *Mr Gumpy's Outing* with their teacher. They discover that the information they need to help them make sense of the story is not there in the book and must instead be taken from their own lives and knowledge of the way the world works. They need to know about floating and sinking, about deep and shallow water, about the fear of drowning; they also need to know about common sense and wisdom and fair play in order to be able to read the story in a way that makes sense. Most of all they need the time and space to discuss their ideas. Their teacher recognises this and responds to what they are doing. She pauses in her reading for them to comment on what's happened (p. 71):

ANTHONY: It was a big boat that was. He shouldn't have let them in.
TEACHER: I hope they could all swim.
ANTHONY: I think so.
REID: The cat won't be able to.
TEACHER: Won't it?
ANTHONY: Cats can't swim.

The teacher's role is to respond to these initiatives and allow the children to make these kind of judgements, even though they may change the words of the original story; the teacher is not in the business of judging correctness but of empowering the children by allowing speculation and exploration of this kind. Most importantly, of course, her role is never punitive. After the initial discussion she invites the children to interpret the meaning they are making in more detail. She does this by making a comment that is intended to help them to build an image that holds the story together and weaves meaning into it:

TEACHER: Perhaps the water won't be too deep. Perhaps their feet will reach the bottom.
REID: The other day I went to a swimming baths and I had a seat in a canoe boat with me and I went in a massive ... I went in first the children's boat and then the mummy and daddy's boat and there was a deep end and a little end.
TEACHER: A deep end and a shallow end was it?

The teacher gives Reid the opportunity to reflect on the central idea of the story and apply it in a way that he finds helpful. She knows that the meaning of *Mr Gumpy's Outing* does not lie in the pages of a book but needs to be remade by Reid himself, with her help; and because of the way she interacts with him he knows this too. Later, as he begins to read independently, he will be able to use this model of learning for himself and his independent reading will involve him in silent conversations about ideas and experiences from his world knowledge and from his own life.

One way in which Gurdeep's teacher encourages him to use what he already knows is by focusing on the words of the story, reading a phrase and pausing while he completes it (p. 13):

TEACHER: 'So Goldilocks climbed up on to the very big bed but it was too ... '
GURDEEP: Lumpy.
TEACHER: 'Too lumpy. Then she climbed on to the medium-sized bed but it was too ... '
GURDEEP: Smooth.

Reid's mother sets up a similar situation for him, telling him explicitly what she wants him to do (p. 68):

MOTHER: I want you to help me remember what they all wanted now. 'The mouse had ... '
REID: Cheese.
MOTHER: 'and the dog had a ... '
REID: Bone.
MOTHER: 'Jane had ... '
REID: Cake.

Reid and Gurdeep could not have read these two passages alone, but by completing the phrases they are being given another way of taking part in the retelling of the story, with the crucial support of the adult reader.

Adult experienced readers consciously and unconsciously act as reading 'models' for young children, and because children learn from adults they wish to emulate, adult reading behaviour is important for children to observe. Gurdeep watches his mother read the Guru Granth Saheb, Reid sees his father looking up a reference to an insect, Gemma observes her father doing the crossword. The children see their future reading biographies already written in the behaviour of older members of their family who show them what it will be like for them when they are older. At school the children see their teachers read their own books during reading time. Skilled readers who show what it's like to be a reader, show them ways of holding different books, of reading silently and alone or in a group, with companions. They demonstrate what kinds of choices are to be made about reading. They also show children the whole task complete – whether it's reading the newspaper, finishing a story, reading a prayer, looking up a reference; in other words, the child knows what to aim for because they have seen the whole operation through.[6]

Often, too, children can become each other's teachers; the children in this study are capable of sharing a book together, without adult intervention, and learning from each other.[7] Gemma and Geeta's version of *The Three Bears* illustrates this well:

GEMMA: Porridge was too hot and they set off out in the woods. Long time ago. Her name was Goldilocks. Don't know this bit.

GEETA: Once upon a time there was Goldilocks. She came in and she and she's nearly open the door and nobody was there. I got that book.

GEMMA: Too sweet said Goldilocks. Daddy bear ... too hot. Tries mummy bear. Too lumpy. Tries mummy bear ... tries baby bear ... the best, so baby bear now just right. So she ate it all up. Don't know it.

GEETA: She she sitting in baby chair and she crashed. Really sorry. She sitting ...

GEMMA: I know it. She went upstairs and she tries daddy's bed. Too high. Tried mummy's bed. Too high. Tried mummy's bed. Too ...

GEETA: Lumpy.

GEMMA: Lumpy. Tries baby bear's bed. Just right.

I wrote earlier (p. 26) that these two girls make learning happen for each other in a context set up by their teacher. They are free to read the story at their own pace, to take control of their learning, and to 'play' at being readers – a kind of rehearsal for when they can read independently. We need to take account of the importance of children learning together like this, taking over the teacher's role for each other, helping, supporting, giving information. Gemma and Geeta clearly benefit from being an audience for each other and jointly creating the meaning of this story. Neither child could have produced this retelling independently. The nature of this kind of learning can surely be regarded as an important resource for the teacher, who can set up an environment for reading and play where this kind of collaboration can happen.

Adult experienced readers who have the task of helping young children to read need to be critical of the reading material that is offered to children and sensitive to the processes which help children to become readers. This chapter has shown that they must also be concerned with the way in which they collaborate with their young readers. They must help young readers to do something more difficult than they would be able to achieve on their own, and they need to do this by providing reading material sufficiently difficult to create interest (this includes rereading favourite books and finding something new within their pages – a comment perhaps, or an idea) and then permitting the child to ask their own questions and make their own comments. The result of this collaboration is that the child is enabled to do things an adult reader does and so gets the same satisfaction from the task. The adult's skill lies in knowing how much the child can do, how much support to give, and where the differences lie. The child too has an active part to play in this kind of interaction; without their active engagement such collaboration would be impossible. The child has to learn to take part in a conversation about a book, to bring thoughts and share ideas from their own life, to trust the adult with those thoughts, to ask questions, to know how to be a listener. The result is the kind of collaborative good practice demonstrated by the children and adults in this chapter.

Pathways to Reading

In Chapters 6 and 7 I looked at the kinds of things children already know about reading and explored the importance of story in their lives; the last chapter described the ways in which their reading is supported in partnership with a skilled reader. It has been necessary to document these events and experiences because they form an integral part of the children's early reading histories, but in concentrating my own attention on them I am conscious that I might unwittingly have imposed a kind of uniformity on the children's early reading experiences. This was not my intention; such a uniformity cannot exist because even though certain learning patterns are shared they are nevertheless enmeshed in the social and cultural traditions of each child's family and community and are subject to their particular values and beliefs.[1]

Before the children started school they were already part of their own reading and writing networks. They had observed, or been included in, the reading and writing activities of their home and neighbourhood; the print they saw around them had given them information about what people use written language for – and their attitudes towards it. Gurdeep sees these signs above his head as he enters the temple:

ਮਰਦਾਨਾ ਜੁਤੀਆਂ   ਜਨਾਨਾ ਜੁਤੀਆਂ

Men's shoes   Ladies' shoes

These notices not only carry factual statements about where to put your shoes; they also carry cultural messages about traditions and appropriateness which Gurdeep keys into and interacts with. This example shows us that language is not just a system; it is the medium for transmitting the social and cultural life of the community, and Gurdeep is inserted into it from birth.

The children's reading biographies document the kinds of reading and writing that form part of their everyday lives: print that is to do with shopping, recipes, sending off for things; looking up information in books, or checking stolen car numbers, reading and studying a sacred text; watching parents doing accounts and writing letters; the ritual of the bedtime story.[2] And we have seen that they are also already part of a wider network of media literacy, mainly through watching television and videos.[3] In addition, nursery and play-group experience have given them opportunities of using story through play and of listening to stories. But of course these experiences are not equally shared; the children have a different range of experiences, rooted in the way of living of their particular family and its community. They will arrive at school with their own unique identities as language users and their own notions of what reading is about; and they will bring their own knowledge to the task of learning to read.

The parents in this study have views on learning based on their own social and cultural beliefs and traditions. They have been their child's teachers from birth, and also careful observers of their child's learning and growth. Gemma's mother remembers how they helped her learn to walk (p. 25):

> I used to sit at one end and her dad used to sit a bit nearer and I used to say, 'Come on', and we used to do it for hours. She wasn't long walking.

and to talk:

> We'd say everything we'd seen, like. I think 'dog' was quite a quick word with her because she liked dogs. Then 'nan' and 'grandad'. She seemed to pick them up. She more or less learned herself.

Anthony's mother explains how she helped him learn to talk (p. 38):

> I just let it come on its own 'cos it's better that way. They sort of pick up things here and there. If you push them too much it takes longer. They lose interest in what you're trying to tell them.

Reid's mother defines learning philosophy as follows (p. 62):

> We look for the learning potential in everything. We believe in spending time constructively and creatively as a way of preparing the children for life.

Parents, of course, have expectations for their children, and this includes the notion of doing well at school. Gemma's mother is prepared to support her daughter at school:

> I'd like Gemma to get something, not just go into a factory like I did (p. 18) ... we'll have to get some more decent books. I'll be reading with her now she's starting school. Now she's old enough to appreciate it. (p. 19)

Anthony's mother and sister also have expectations for him (p. 37):

> I think school will change him a lot.
> I keep on telling him, 'You've got to go to school in September', and he's still running about in the garden.

The parents are careful observers, too, of how their children respond to print:

> When Gurdeep was a baby you'd be reading or writing and he'd be out there sitting in that corner and quickly he would pick it up. (p. 7).

> Geeta doesn't know the ABC but she still brings a book. (p. 50)

> Geeta tries to read according to the pictures. (p. 50)

These views on reading and learning haven't suddenly arrived from nowhere; they are part of a set of beliefs about learning that have developed within the family, or been remembered from school days. It is in comments like these that the parents communicate the value they place on literacy and the approaches to learning they feel are right for their child, and these approaches are going to differ according to the family's views on learning and on what is being read. Gurdeep starts out along the pathway to religious literacy:

> Gurdeep sits with me and he wants to touch the holy book. I tell him the words are in Punjabi. (p. 10)

Anthony's mother concentrates on helping him to understand the story. It's not important to her at this point that he should recognise or remember words. She knows too that the illustrations will help him to make sense of the story. She reads the book through first:

> ... so he gets the whole sort of picture of it and then we go back through the book and I say to him, 'What's happening there?' ... then he can tell me everything that's happening, before it's happened ... You just can't read to him. You've got to hold the book so he can see the pictures. (p. 38)

Gemma's mother reads to her daughter and encourages Gemma to respond:

> When you're reading her stories she takes it all in. 'Cos if I read the book over again to her she's telling me what's coming on the page. On one book she says, 'and he told her off' and before I turn the page over she knew it was on the next page. (p. 25)

Reid's mother has a clear view of how she likes to share a book with him so that he will learn and enjoy the story at the same time. She controls the story-reading session carefully by eliciting certain responses from Reid at certain points in the story and often looks ahead to pinpoint certain strategies she can use to help him understand (p. 65).

Sharing a book with a child is a form of social interaction, involving a cultural transmission of attitudes, values, beliefs and skills. There is nothing 'natural' or, indeed, universal about any of these reading practices between parents and their children. The idea of reading aloud to a child is not one that is practised by all parents as a matter of course (Gemma's mother will begin to read with her when she comes to school; Geeta's parents are far too busy running their sewing factory to be able to read with their daughter).[4] Reid's parents, who regularly read bedtime stories to him, were both read to themselves as children and place a high value on the enjoyment of stories. They have remained readers all their lives and so, though they may not realise it, reading aloud to Reid is a cultural practice influenced by their way of life. So, too, is the way in which they share a book with Reid. He is included in conversations and decision-making at home about all kinds of things that relate to the family, and this kind of interaction is evident in storytime sessions like this one when he and his mother share *That Fat Cat* together (p. 67):

MOTHER: He wants to have loads and loads. A bit like you then isn't he, really?
REID: No.
MOTHER: Oh well, you have loads and loads of dinner, don't you?
REID: I don't have loads and loads of ice cream.
MOTHER: Don't you? You're always saying to me ... what do you say?
REID: I want a sweetie!
MOTHER: So you're a bit like Kafka. You might get fat like him if you eat like you do.

There is nothing natural about learning to take meaning from a book in this way; it is learned behaviour, and Reid will no doubt read with his own children in much the same way. In contrast, Gurdeep's reading time with his own father is of a totally different order (p. 14). His father is concerned to see that his children learn about Indian culture through the book they share, and he says, 'I stop and see if there's a hard word I think they might not have understood'.[5] In fact he appears more comfortable reading to the children than eliciting a conversation about the story with them, and in Chapter 1 I hypothesise that since he is used to taking the role of active listener himself at the temple, he may now see his own role as mediator of the story when he reads to his children, who in turn become listeners.

When parents read with their children they often choose to read stories. But which stories do they choose? And why? These questions have been brought to our attention recently by Shirley Brice Heath,[6] who lived and worked with two communities of people, one white, one Black, in the Piedmont Carolinas: Roadville and Trackton. Her accounts of spontaneous storytelling in the two distinct communities highlights narrative differences for us. For the people of Roadville, stories have to be accounts of actual events that have happened; fictional stories count as lies. Their stories also have to have a moral theme. 'Children in Roadville', Brice Heath tells us,

> are not allowed to tell stories, unless an adult announces that something which happened to a child makes a good story and invites a retelling. When children are asked to retell such events, they are expected to tell non-fictive stories which 'stick to the truth'.[7]

In contrast the people of Trackton are exuberant storytellers and though they might use an actual event as the basis for a story, 'they creatively fictionalise the details surrounding the real event, and the outcome of the story may not even resemble what indeed happened'.[8] Their stories do not have the function of controlling through moral example; they need to be dramatic and powerful, to combine wild fantasy with reality. Brice Heath tells us: 'In short, for Roadville, Trackton's stories would be lies; for Trackton, Roadville's stories would not even count as stories.'[9]

The stories Gurdeep's mother tells are embedded in a cultural practice she learned as a child in India, and in telling stories to her son she holds firmly to her roots and her cultural identity. The moral tale she tells about the tortoise (p. 11) is designed to give an important message to its listeners, in this case instructing Gurdeep how he is expected to behave. Again, there is nothing 'natural' about the way his mother tells the tale. It is a created cultural form, culturally given.[10] Stories like this are handed down by grandparents, parents, teachers and priests, and help us to understand ourselves and our position in the society we live in. The context of the story, of course, has changed now: Gurdeep will not be able to listen to it sleeping under the stars in India as his mother did; and now that she has told it to us at school and it has been written down and given permanence in this book, for a new audience, its context has changed yet again.

Gurdeep also learns about his place in the family and in society when he hears his mother tell a story concerning his possible future: 'We teach them from the beginning because we always live together and we're expecting the same thing from them when we get older and they have to live with us and look after us.' Gurdeep constructs himself through the stories he is told about himself. When he looks back on his life through his photographs from babyhood onwards he is able to give himself a picture of his world and tell the story of his own life (p. 9). In telling this story he becomes the author of his own childhood, the storyteller of his own past, incorporating memory into story and creating not only a personal biography but a story about himself that is social, cultural and historical because it has its roots intertwined in cultural history. His life story is illuminated for him by his parents and Gurdeep learns to tell a story about himself that places him comfortably within his family traditions.

At home Gurdeep reads *The Naughty Mouse* and learns not to be naughty himself. At school there are only a few books of fables and most of the stories belong to the tradition of Western Europe.[11] One of these is *Goldilocks and the Three Bears*, and towards the end of his first year in school Gurdeep wanted to hear this particular story over and over again. It was now his favourite story and, interestingly, it does not follow the narrative form of the fairy tale; in fact, in some ways it is more akin to the moral tale – Goldilocks does something wrong and receives her punishment. She is frightened by the bears and worried in case her mother finds out what she's done: thus there is no happy ending and nothing is resolved. We are not even told if Goldilocks is repentant.[12] Does Gurdeep like this story so much, I wonder, because he implicitly recognises within it elements from both the fairy tale and the moral tale? He certainly has a particularly rich experience of the narrative form of two cultures.

As well as fairy tales, Gurdeep's classroom library also has a fair number of picture-story books on the shelves and even though these are beautiful books – 'real' books, as some of us have come to describe them [13]– we must nevertheless remember that they are not culture-free. There are underlying cultural assumptions behind the construction of the picture-story books which the children read in the classroom. These books are not culturally neutral; they presuppose a particular way of reading by an adult and an apprentice child reader. Their words, design and illustrations are fashioned to enable young readers and their adult helpers to talk about the meaning of the story in a conversational style. Some invite readers to repeat the formula over and over again (think of 'and he went rumpeta, rumpeta, rumpeta all the way down the road', from *The Elephant and the Bad Baby*). Others encourage the shared expression of laughter at awkward situations (think of what happens to the fox in *Rosie's Walk*). Yet others help children to connect with other stories (think of all the well-known stories embedded in *The Jolly Postman* or *Each Peach Pear Plum*). Picture books without words, like *The Snowman*, need to have their stories constructed afresh at each reading by adult and child.

Authors are writing books like these within a specific cultural framework and with a particular audience in mind – notably the hypothetical child reader who is socialised into responding to a story by making a conversation out of it. Their books are presented in ways which encourage the child to ask questions about the story, to predict what will happen next and to match what does happen against experiences in their own lives; the books require them to investigate and use their imagination, to stop and discuss and to interpret the words of the author.[14] This presupposes a way of reading which is not shared by everyone and tensions can be set up between child, teacher and parent if there is a cultural mismatch about the way in which a book is to be read and understood by a child.

The reading material in schools, whether it consists of reading primers, annuals, labels, picture-story books, notices, comics, writing on the blackboard, a school magazine or newsletter, dual-language books, folk tales, fables, letters home to parents, dictionaries, home-made books, and so on, is not culturally neutral. Teachers and schools work from a cultural base too, and teachers hold sets of beliefs about learning to read. Geeta, Gemma, Gurdeep, Reid and Anthony have shown us that schools do not hold a monopoly on reading and writing or on beliefs about literacy.[15] But for these children the school is the common cultural link, the base from which they do a great deal of reading and writing, some of which is shared with their parents. To help them and many other children like them to become literate in the fullest sense, we need now to set up total literacy environments for our children, which embrace the views of parents, teachers and children and encompass learning in the home, the community and the school.

I began this study three years ago in order to find out more about the process of learning to read at home and at school. My brief glimpse into the pre-school lives and literacies of Gemma, Gurdeep, Anthony, Reid and Geeta has enabled me to see that any reading a child encounters in school always has a previous history. The children did not arrive at school illiterate: each brought with them reading experiences of their own, learned socially in collaboration with others. Formally described, these are to do with learning about narrative, listening to stories, developing a sense of the book, especially a sacred text, learning names of products from media advertising and food labels, reciting jingles and jokes and seeing book-reading and writing modelled by parents and others in the family and community. Each of these literacy experiences interacts with the total lifestyle of the families and each contains within it an unspoken assumption about print and its functions, which I have tried to make explicit through the children's reading biographies and the discussion which followed.

When the five children arrived at school they all brought with them distinct views of reading and writing which came up against the school view in a new social environment. Schools in general are perhaps not as aware as they should be of these early experiences of literacy. In order to become conscious of pre-school experiences and their differences and to add a social dimension to our knowledge of the reading process, we need to give ourselves a new way of looking at what children might be doing when they come to school at the age of four. At present we know little about the knowledge of reading they bring to school with them, and still less about what parents might have done to help their children learn to read – in spite of their involvement in home-school reading projects. Our knowledge of the cultural beliefs and values of families and their effect on children as readers has to be made a professional concern. Specifically we need a detailed knowledge of the kinds of literacies available to a child and the ways the child is socialised into responding, including ways of sharing books. Only by acquiring this will we know how a child views the task of learning to read when he or she enters school.

Teachers and parents must set up a two-way flow of information, with teachers sharing their more developed expertise with parents, and parents sharing with teachers their knowledge about the kinds of literacies they offer to children, including ways of sharing books. This action would help to give parents confidence by making them conscious of their own hidden skills. At present many parents expect professionals to construct their role for them within the school setting.

Children become part of a new social group when they enter school, and bring with them views of themselves as learners. It is crucial that the school helps build on that view by showing children that their pre-school experience is valid and significant, and finding ways of reflecting it back to them. Teachers can no longer think in terms of a single standardised schooled literacy which functions irrespective of the child's background; there must be acknowledgement that the experience of literacy is inseparable from the experience of family life.

Children take reading experiences from school to home for their parents to share; it is therefore important that the school's view of literacy is made explicit for parents, so that both parents and teachers can work together in full knowledge of what the other is doing. It is too easy for the school view of literacy to diminish the child as a learner by ignoring, or having no knowledge of, previously acquired competencies. The school that uses basal readers, for example, takes no account of the child who has learned a complex set of reading lessons through sharing picture-story books at home. The school must therefore make explicit for itself its own unspoken assumptions about print and literacy as it is taught and used in the school. Twenty years ago James Britton wrote:

> ... in school we cannot afford to ignore all that has gone on before. So often in the past we have tried to make a fresh start, at the risk of cutting off the roots which alone can sustain the growth we look for. It is not only that the classroom must more and more merge into the ·orld outside it, but that the processes of school learning must merge into the processes of learning that begin at birth and are life-long. We can no longer regard school learning as simply an interim phase, a period of instruction and apprenticeship that marks the change from immaturity to maturity, from play in the nursery to work in the world. School learning must both build upon the learning of infancy

and foster something that will continue and evolve through adult life. (1970, p.129)

If anything, these words are more relevant today than they were in the 1970s. For Gemma, Gurdeep, Geeta, Reid, Anthony and countless other children, learning to read will continue and evolve through adult life if the processes of learning in school and in the community keep in touch with each other.

Three years on ...

Gurdeep

Gurdeep tells me he can't remember how he learned to read: 'I just started reading,' he says. His teacher agrees that it happened that way for him too. Gurdeep's parents feel he is 'doing really well' now. They say he never asks them for help with difficult words but prefers to figure them out for himself. 'I divide them and make the sounds,' he tells me. He is pleased to be reading 'hard books' and says that the first long book he read was *The Owl Who Was Afraid of the Dark*, which his teacher had just read to the whole class. 'I read the whole book,' he says. At quiet reading time he likes to sit at his table with his back to everyone else, privately. He reads for half an hour at a time and often carries on reading when the reading time is over.

Gurdeep visits the library every fortnight and chooses his own books. 'It doesn't take him five minutes to choose six,' says his mother. I notice that some of the books he has chosen are picture-story books (*Gorilla* is one of them), though he tells me he prefers 'hard books with little words'. His mother makes sure he reads one of his library books and the book he brings from school each day, and although he prefers reading to himself – 'then I don't get disturbed' – his mother asks him to read aloud at times because 'we still want to listen to him in case he is pronouncing the words wrong'. His father and older sister occasionally read to him but his mother now has no time to tell him Indian folk tales, 'though I talk to the children about the religious stories of the Gurus and Gurdeep knows the names of the ten Gurus now'. Gurdeep goes to Punjabi classes at the temple on Sunday and reads tales of the Gurus in Punjabi, and then in English, and his teacher asks him questions to see if he has understood. He has his own copy of a beginners' alphabet book in Punjabi. He is given responsibility for helping to sort the money at the temple.

Transformers no longer feature in Gurdeep's life. His skateboard, his football and his yo-yo are among his most treasured possessions and he reads the yo-yo instruction sheet to learn new tricks. He has a computer and uses it to write with or to play games. He likes to write on the word-processor at school because 'your hand doesn't get sore'. Gurdeep watches television a great deal and sings along with the advertisements. His favourite programmes are 'Bugs Bunny', 'Cities of Gold', 'Dallas', the Lenny Henry show and the Cosby show.

Gemma

'I can read *Teddy Bear Postman*,' says Gemma. She opens the book with confidence and her eyes turn directly to the print. Her favourite stories, she says, are *Are You My Mother?* and *Dogger*. She is still reading at home with her mother, who says, 'I think she's done well. For her age. I'm pleased.' Gemma asks her mother for paper 'all the time' and spends a lot of time writing. She asks her mother for help spelling words and does sums which she asks her mother to mark. Gemma is far more self-assured, though she still needs reassurance at times: she is hesitant about writing and needs to know that each word is correct before she commits it to paper. Her younger sister, Jade, often comes into her classroom and they read together and sometimes write. She often tells her mother about things she's done at school.

Gemma can recognise food labels now and she is very interested in the offers on cereal packets. Her favourite television programmes are 'Home and Away' and 'Neighbours' – she has a picture of Jason from 'Neighbours' on her bedroom wall. She also likes cartoons and films on video. Gemma always wants to help her mother and offers to go shopping, or tidy up, or dry the pots. Her teacher is pleased that 'she knows what reading's all about, and though she still needs support I don't think she'll be long before she reads on her own'.

Anthony

Anthony still likes the story of *Little Red Riding Hood*. 'I tell it to myself at night in my mind, in my sleep,' he tells me. 'I can't remember all the book. I can only remember in the woods. The wolf comes first, then Little Red Riding Hood comes.' He has a few books of his own, too, like *Superman Monthly*, which he bought at Asda when he was shopping with his mum. 'It's about evil and good,' he says. 'Dark Storm is evil and the other one's good. The Cheetah is good but he ain't the leader. The lion's the leader, and I've got the little animal, like a Cheetah, and you can move the legs. Fast-medium-slow speeds.'

Anthony loves watching films on video. One evening recently he saw *Three Men and a Baby*. His mother said he liked it so much that he watched it all through again the following morning on his own. He starts to tell me the story: 'It's about three men. They can't look after the baby properly and the lady holds him ... '

Anthony says he likes reading ''cos you can read to someone and if you've got a baby brother you can read your book to them when you get older. One day I got my reading book. I sat my brother down beside me and I read it to him.' His mother says he seems frightened to say words he's reading in case he's wrong. At school we sit and read together. He chooses John Burningham's *Granpa* and points to the word 'sunshine'. 'That's one whole word,' he tells me. He points to 'tomorrow' and asks, 'Is that a whole word?' Then he turns the pages with confidence and his eyes follow the print as we read. 'There's the girl speaking,' he says, pointing to the text. I ask him how he knows. 'It's posh writing,' he tells me, then he shows me the print that signifies Granpa is speaking to her.

His mother wishes he would read more. His main interest, she says, is in playing out and having sweets. Sometimes she thinks she expects too much of him but at the same time she feels he should do more reading, writing and maths and has restricted his playing-out time so that he does some book work in the evening after his tea. He doesn't seem to object: 'One day I was going out to play and my mum told me off and said I have to learn. Now I do some work. Like sums and times tables. It's good 'cos then you can learn.'

His mother plays Scrabble with Paulette and he tries to join in, but finds it difficult, so she's going to buy him Junior Scrabble and play that with him. His mother doesn't often have time to read with him, but he does pick up books now that Paulette is doing homework regularly. His mother bought a novel from Woolworth's recently – the first she has bought for a long time. 'I could do with reading a good book. I want something to read at work instead of knitting all night when the patients are asleep,' she explains. The novel is about the Deep South.

Anthony remembers he has a Transformer book. It's about Optimus Prime 'when he's very little'. He tells me the story:

> One day he went out in his truck and he went to this place and he didn't know the baddies lived there and they caught him. He thought the place he went to was the baddies but it was the goodies, then he stayed with the proper goodies, then he grew up. Then he turned into a truck. Then he became a leader. And that's it.

Geeta

Geeta still loves listening to stories at school and her favourite story at the moment is *Meg and Mog*. She mixes well and likes to use her knowledge of language and reading to 'play teacher' with a group of children, telling them a story or at other times leaning over their shoulders when they are reading to prompt them if they are stuck on a word. Her teacher says she knows a great deal about books and is very interested in the alphabetic nature of written language. Even so, she is not yet able to trust herself to read independently, though her teacher feels the knowledge she needs is there in her head. She is fascinated by the keyboard on the word-processor and loves to study it. 'How do you get a capital letter?' she asked her teacher recently.

Her mother says Geeta can read if she concentrates but she 'makes silly mistakes'. She believes children are motivated to learn either through fear or through jealousy, and that Geeta has not yet been motivated sufficiently in either of these areas to want to learn. She spends a great deal of time at home colouring, mostly houses and people, and says she wants to be a wrestler when she grows up. Her older brother writes sums out for her and Ranu still reads with her, though she doesn't have so much time now that she has more homework. Geeta's older brother and sisters all had private tuition from an Indian teacher who taught them 'English and grammar' and Geeta is beginning lessons with this teacher too. This will mean she has no time to go to the library.

Geeta still loves cartoons, which she watches on the children's channel of cable television. Mickey Mouse is her favourite. She also likes watching the Cosby show, 'Home and Away' and 'Neighbours'. 'If she hears a song once on TV, she's got it,' her mother says, but she really feels that Geeta watches too much television. The family view Indian films on video and are particularly interested in the cycle of Hindu films of the Gita. Geeta is not yet interested in religious books but her mother is not anxious about this and feels she is still 'too young to look at the books, though she knows about Rama and Sita'.

Reid

Reid chooses his own books from the library once a month, though his mother steps in to guide him if he chooses books that are far too hard. She says he's very interested in books with photographs in, books about everyday things like going shopping, and dual-language books about Asian children (this is probably because he has been learning Punjabi at school). Recently he has begun choosing books about diving and says he wants to be a diver when he grows up – he watches anything on television to do with diving. Reid has a comic each week called *Number One* and he also enjoys 'books that do things' like pop-up books. He owns his own Question books on Myths and Legends and Birds and Butterflies and these help him when the family do quizzes together – he is particularly knowledgeable about nature quizzes. His parents say he still 'loves *The Snowman*' and likes to listen to the tape of the story set to music.

Reid idolises Michael Jackson and enjoys his *Moonwalker* book. 'He has a go at quite difficult words,' his mother explains, though she notices that at other times he uses the illustrations to help him sort out the meaning. At school he uses picture cues too and 'tries to sound out difficult words' – he finds this strategy helpful. He reads in bursts, both at home and at school; sometimes he's very interested in a book but at other times he 'can't be bothered' reading. He still has a bedtime story but these days, instead of being read to all the time by his father, they share the reading more; and sometimes he sits down and reads to himself while he waits for his father to come into his bedroom. 'He whispers the words aloud,' his father observes.

Reid is a confident writer and uses his knowledge of letter-sounds to help him with his invented spellings. His mother worries about his mirror-writing and wonders if it is because he is left-handed. He recently sat down at home and wrote a long letter to a little girl he is fond of. She used to be in his class but has now left the area.

Notes

Part One: Five Children

1 Gurdeep

1. A version of this chapter entitled 'Learning to Read at Home and at School' appeared in *English in Education* (vol. 22, no. 3). Copyright 1988, National Association for the Teaching of English. Reprinted with permission.

2 Gemma

1. A version of this chapter entitled 'Teacher Inquiry in the Classroom: "Read It To Me Now!"' appeared in *Language Arts* (April 1988). Copyright 1988, National Council of Teachers of English. Reprinted with permission.

Part Two: Further Considerations

6 Learning to Read

1. Carol Fox (1983) studied children's oral monologues in order to discover what contribution written stories made towards an emergent literary competence, and drew the conclusion that children learn complex rules of narrative production before they can read and write. These rules, she says, are ones 'which we are sometimes more accustomed to find underlying the texts of more mature adult writers'.

2. Marilyn Cochran-Smith (1986) defines the reader-as-spokesperson-for-text as a person who is 'translating from the written to the oral channel' and gives as examples a Congressman presenting a statement to the legislature, or a minister reading a biblical passage to his or her congregation.

Anthony's mother takes on this role when she reads to him, expecting that he will listen to her attentively.

3. Jean-Paul Sartre (1964) tells of his growing bewilderment as his mother read to him one day with a 'plaster voice'. Where was her own voice that he knew? Her familiar words and phrases? After a while he realised that it was the book that was talking, not his mother; she had taken over the voice on the page.

4. Cliff Moon (1988) argues convincingly for a learning model in which the child completes the whole act of reading first before beginning to learn about isolated reading skills: 'Learning to read, like learning to swim, walk or ride a bike, is a question of completing the whole act first, however imperfectly and approximately, and refining the parts later through experience and practice.'

5. For a more detailed consideration of this important area, see D.W. Harding (1967). The author suggests that evaluation of characters and events is a central psychological activity on the part of the reader; not only does the reader share in the events of the story, he or she reacts to the characters' behaviour as much as with them. Harding goes on to suggest that it is only in 'successful fiction' that the reader is encouraged to behave in this way.

6. James Britton (1970) writes at length on the roles of participant and spectator, building on the work of D.W. Harding (1937).

7. Margaret Spencer (1980) writes of 'the retreat into the alternative world' of the book, which provides an opportunity for some children to withdraw from the world for a time and engage with their imagination and emotions. Other children find this possibility too frightening, preferring to keep both feet firmly anchored in the social world of friendship and joint activity.

8. 'The most curious thing about a fully literate person', Margaret Meek (1982) reminds us, 'is that he knows what he needn't read. Good readers are secure in the knowledge that no one reads everything.'

9. Brian Street (1984) suggests that the concepts of format, layout and page design of books are 'hidden' literacy skills that English children pick up from their parents while their parents imagine they are teaching them different ones. He uses research from the Adult Literacy and Basic Skills Unit to support his argument.

10. Margaret Meek (1988) discusses many of the implicit reading lessons children have learned for themselves. She concludes:

Teachers are naturally concerned about what people have to learn and their responsibility for teaching these things, so they sometimes undervalue what the children have already discovered about writing and reading. If there is no place or chance for beginners to demonstrate what they can do, what they know will never be part of their teachers' awareness.

11. The technical term used to describe language to talk about language is 'metalanguage', and Simons and Murphy (1986) define it like this:

Metalinguistic awareness is the ability to focus on the language itself as an object rather than on the meaning or the intention of the communication. It allows language users to focus attention on the phonological, lexical, syntactic, semantic, and pragmatic levels of language, to notice anomalies at these different linguistic levels, and to comment on them.

12. Reid (1966) and Downing (1969) concluded from their research that children who were slow to read could not recognise terms like 'sentence', 'word', 'letter', or 'sound' and that, conversely, children who could understand these metalinguistic terms were successful in learning to read. Clark (1976) also discovered that most of the children in her study who read fluently before they came to school were familiar with the terms 'word', 'letter' and 'sentence'. However, much depends on what is meant by 'learning to read'. If decoding is seen as the central skill, then metalinguistic awareness may be of central importance. This chapter has shown that a great deal of learning about reading precedes sound-symbol recognition. It seems safer to assume, therefore, that metalinguistic awareness develops as a part of the whole reading process.

13. Margaret Meek (1982) writes of the joke:

It is a complete story, a verbal trick, another example of how we separate meaning from words. Part of the ritual of jokes is joining in the game of telling them, or asking riddles even before you know exactly why it is funny or how the trick works.

7 Entering Fairyland

1. Ruth Weir (1962) discusses in fascinating detail the pre-sleep monologues of her son, Anthony. She recorded him as he talked himself to sleep every night between the ages of two years four months and two years six months and found that although he was of course monologuing, he was having conversations with 'companions' and entering an imaginary world in his head.

2. Vygotsky (1978) describes play as desire: 'an imaginary, illusory world in which the unrealisable tendencies can be realised' (p. 93). His chapter 'The Role of Play in Development' is essential reading for anyone interested in any aspects of learning through play and in making links between imaginative play, cognitive development and the psychological process of reading.

3. Max's bedroom appears in *Where The Wild Things Are*. Margaret Spencer (1976) acclaims this book as 'one of the most enchanting stories ever told or depicted' and explains that it 'is a symbolic representation of the complicated childhood experience of guilt and restitution'. Her significant essay discusses the gap between children being read to and children reading for themselves, and the importance of the 'storying' children engage in.

4. Elizabeth Cook (1969) discusses the importance of myths, legends and fairy tales in children's lives and describes how they can best be shared with children.

5. Iser (1978) reminds us that reading is not a one-way process from author to reader, but is instead a dynamic interaction between text and reader (p.107). It is the reader who must do the work of building images for the story in order to take meaning from it and make connections between the story and everyday life.

6. Gordon Wells (1985) carried out his research project in Bristol and part of his work led him to track the pre-school learning experiences of children who were successful in the Knowledge of Literacy tests at seven and then again at eleven. He found these children could be identified by one thing: they had had stories told or read to them before they came to school. But why stories and not other activities? Wells hypothesised that in the act of understanding stories children are pushed towards the use of decontextualised language, making meaning from the words alone, and this sustained activity calls for higher levels of cognitive thinking. In the act of listening to stories, he writes,

> the child is beginning to come to grips with the symbolic potential of language, its power to represent experience in symbols which are independent of the objects, events and relationships which are symbolised, and which can be interpreted in contexts other than those in which the experience originally occurred. (p.134)

When children are required to operate at higher cognitive levels in their school work they are clearly at an advantage if they have had experience of making meaning from decontextualised language which they have met at an early age through story.

7. Holdaway (1979) is in no doubt that children who have a pre-school background of book experience have a significant advantage over those who do not, for they:

> are able to attend to language without reference to the immediate situation around them, and respond to it in complex ways by creating images from their past experiences – they have learned to operate vicariously. This has opened a new dimension of fantasy and imagination, allowing them to create images of things never experienced or entities which do not exist in the real world. By these means they are able to escape from the bonds of the present into the past and the future. (p. 49)

8 Reading Partnerships

1. This chapter discusses the way in which skilled readers help young children to become more competent at reading. This process of helping children learn is based firmly within a Vygotskian model of learning and development. Vygotsky (1978) believes that the pathway to learning lies in what he calls the 'zone of proximal development', which he defines in this way:

> It is the distance between the actual developmental level as determined by independent problem solving and the level of potential development as determined through problem solving under adult guidance or in collaboration with more capable peers. (p. 86)

In this chapter, adult experienced readers who are responsible for helping a child learn to read enter their zone of proximal development by supporting them as they read books which they would not be able to read independently and by acting as 'reading models' for young children to imitate. The children in this study who ask questions about the stories they read, and make comments which relate to their own lives, are positioning themselves within their own zone of proximal development: they know where they wish their learning to lead and therefore need to be listened to with care.

2. Many of these important features are described by Dombey (1988) in the story-reading sessions of Mrs G., a nursery teacher. Mrs G. helps the children to understand the meaning of a book by giving 'a large measure

of control over that meaning to the children in front of her' (p. 80). She does this by responding to all the children's comments she considers relevant and 'by her words and her actions she models for the children how a reader sets about this business' of understanding (p. 80).

Cochran-Smith (1986) also tells of a community in which story-readings were 'joint ventures' between the reader and the child listeners. She documents clearly the active and flexible role of the story-reader and the learning accomplished by the children.

3. The technical term used by Bruner (1978) and others to describe this kind of interaction is 'scaffolding'. It is based on Vygotsky's 'zone of proximal development' (see note 1 above) and involves the adult initially taking responsibility for the reading task and gradually allowing the child to take over more of the reading, with as much support as necessary. In a later article (1985) Bruner defines scaffolding as 'reducing the number of degrees of freedom that the child must manage in the task' (p. 29).

4. Cochran-Smith (1986) discusses the responsibility the story-reader has to translate from the written to the oral mode for the children. She writes:

> To mediate the storyreader had to continuously assess and interpret both the text (e.g. its lexical and syntactic structures, its storyline, temporal and spatial sequences, amount and kind of information carried by the pictures and by the words and the interrelationships of these two kinds of information) and the sense that the listeners were making of all of these. Listeners' sense-making was monitored by the reader's paying close attention to the responses of the listeners. (p. 44)

If you wish to read more about the skill of story-reading to groups of young children, I urge you to read this chapter.

5. See Chapter 9 for more discussion of this point.

6. Bruner (1985) writes that the first task of the adult is 'to model the task, to establish that something is possible and interesting' (p. 29). The second task is to induce the child to try out the task for him- or herself.

7. Forman and Cazden (1985) have made a study of older children teaching younger ones (peer-tutoring) and children of the same age learning alongside each other (peer interaction). They feel that learning between children without an adult is especially important because it forms 'the only context in which children can reverse interactional roles with the same intellectual content, giving directions as well as following them, and asking questions as well as answering them' (p. 344). These teaching relationships between children happen both in the home and at school, and

the authors point out that 'they may be especially important in school because of limitations and rigidities characteristic of adult–child interactions in that institutional setting' (p. 344).

9 Pathways to Reading

1. Bruner (1986) writes:

> Some years ago I wrote some very insistent articles about the importance of discovery learning – learning on one's own ... What I am proposing here is an extension of that idea, or better, a completion. My model of the child in those days was very much in the tradition of the solo child mastering the world by representing it to himself in his own terms. In the intervening years I have come increasingly to recognise that most learning in most settings is a communal activity, the sharing of the culture. It is not just that the child must make his knowledge his own, but that he must make it his own in a community of those who share his sense of belonging to a culture.

2. Anderson and Stokes (1984) move away from the literacy that is to do with story-reading and concentrate on researching and recording literate practices involved in daily living, entertainment and religious activities.
3. Meek (1986) shows how we must not underestimate the emergent literacy skills involved in 'reading television'. Davies (1989) also defends television viewing and her research confirms that pictures are central to children's understanding of the world – something we must take into account when reading picture-story books with children.
4. Reading to children is not a universal practice, and those adults who do read to children do it in remarkably different ways. Shirley Brice Heath (1982) documents the different reading practices of people in Roadville and Trackton in her long study of these two communities of people. In Roadville, a white working-class community in the Piedmont Carolinas, the children do have bedtime stories, but adult readers do not encourage their children to link meanings in books to things that have happened to them or things they know about in the world. Book-reading focuses instead on 'letters of the alphabet, numbers, names of basic items pictured in books, and simplified retellings of stories in the words of the adult' (p. 59). In Trackton, a Black working-class community, there are no bedtime stories and very few occasions when children are specifically read to at all.
5. Shirley Brice Heath (1982) calls our attention to Richard Howard's

statement: 'We require an education in literature ... in order to discover that what we have assumed – with the complicity of our teachers – was nature is in fact culture' (p. 49).

Cochran-Smith (1986) reinforces this view:

> Children ... are not born knowing how to connect their knowledge and experience in 'literate' ways to printed and pictorial texts. Rather, they must learn strategies for understanding texts just as they must learn the ways of eating and talking that are appropriate to their cultures or social groups. (p. 36)

There is nothing 'natural' about Gurdeep's entrance to literacy, whether at home or at school, and it can never be enough to view his growing mastery of literacy as something apart from his whole culture; put another way, any view we have of his literacy learning must be shaped to take account of reading practices both at home and at school.

6. Shirley Brice Heath's book (1983) reads almost like a novel and I recommend it to anyone interested in how different communities of people live in America today, as well as those more specifically interested in how children learn to talk, read and write in different social and cultural settings.

7. Brice Heath (1983), p. 158.

8. ibid., p. 166.

9. ibid., p. 189.

10. Rosen (1984) reminds us:

> ... however universal our human bent for narratising experience, we encounter our own society's modes for doing this. There is no one way of telling stories; we learn the story grammars of our society, our culture. Since there are irreconcilable divisions in our society of sex, class, ethnicity, we should expect very diverse but not mutually exclusive ways of telling stories. The composer of a story is not a completely free agent. (p. 14)

11. Bettelheim (1978) contrasts the moral tale or fable and the fairy tale in this way:

> ... often sanctimonious, sometimes amusing, the fable always explicitly states a moral truth; there is no hidden meaning, nothing is left to our imagination.
>
> The fairy tale, in contrast, leaves all decisions up to us, including whether we wish to make any at all. It is up to us whether we wish to make any application to our life from a fairy tale, or simply enjoy the fantastic events it tells about. Our enjoyment is what induces us to respond in our own good time to the hidden meanings, as they may relate to our life experience and present state of personal development. (pp. 42–3)

12. Bettelheim (1978) analyses the Goldilocks story like this:

> This story lacks some of the most important features of the true fairy tales: at its end there is neither recovery nor consolation; there is no resolution of conflict, and thus no happy ending. (p. 215)

13. See, for example, two excellent booklets which advocate the use of picture-story books for learning to read: Bennett (1979) and Waterland (1988).

14. Cochran-Smith (1986) points out:

> ... the texts and designs of picture books for young children assume, and are directly related to, the adult–child oral language patterns of the social groups that produce and use them. (p. 41)

15. In fact, literacy was not taught in separate institutions called schools until recently, but was acquired in many different social settings, including the home and social and religious groups. Cook-Gumperz (1986) reminds us that:

> The shift from the eighteenth century onwards has not been from total illiteracy to literacy, but from a hard-to-estimate multiplicity of literacies, a pluralistic idea about literacy as a composite of different skills related to reading and writing for many different purposes and sections of a society's population, to a twentieth century notion of a single, standardised, schooled literacy. (p. 22)

Bibliography

Children's Books Referred to in the Text

Ahlberg, J. and A. (1977) *Burglar Bill*. Picture Lions

Ahlberg, J. and A. (1978) *Each Peach Pear Plum*. Kestrel Books

Ahlberg, J. and A. (1986) *The Jolly Postman or Other People's Letters*. Heinemann

Briggs, R. (1978) *The Snowman*. Hamish Hamilton

Browne, A. (1983) *Gorilla*. Magnet

Burningham, J. (1970) *Mr Gumpy's Outing*. Cape

Burningham, J. (1984) *Granpa*. Cape

Carle, E. (1970) *The Very Hungry Caterpillar*. Hamish Hamilton

Eastman, P.D. (1960) *Are You My Mother?* Collins

Evans, E. (1985) *That Fat Cat*. Circle Books

Fassett, J.H. *Beacon Readers*. Ginn & Company Ltd

Frith, M. (1973) *I'll Teach My Dog 100 Words*. Collins

Furchgott, T. (1983) *Nanda in India*. Deutsch

Ginn & Company Ltd (1978) *Ginn 360* Reading Scheme

Hill, E. (1984) *Good Morning Baby Bear*. Heinemann

Hill, P. *The Noisiest Class in School*. Scholastic Publications

Hughes, S. (1977) *Dogger*. The Bodley Head

Hutchins, P. (1968) *Rosie's Walk*. The Bodley Head

Jackson, M. (1988) *Moonwalker*. Heinemann

McKee, D. (1980) *Not Now Bernard*. Andersen Press

Milligan, S. (1968) *Silly Verse For Kids*. Puffin

Nicoll, H. and Pienkowski, J. (1972) *Meg and Mog*. Puffin

Nisbet & Company (1971) *The Kathy and Mark Basic Readers*

O'Donnell, M., Munro, R. and Warwick, M. (1949) *Janet and John*. Reading Scheme. Nisbet & Company

Rosen, M. (1981) *You Can't Catch Me*. Deutsch

Sendak, M. (1970) *Where The Wild Things Are*. Puffin

Smith, D. (1956) *One Hundred and One Dalmatians*. Heinemann

Smith, W.J. 'The Toaster', in *Tiny Tim*. Picture Puffin
Southgate, V. (1971) *Goldilocks and the Three Bears*. Ladybird Books
Southgate, V. (1972) *Little Red Riding Hood*. Ladybird Books
Stone, S. (1985) *The Naughty Mouse*. Luzac Storytellers
Tomlinson, J. (1968) *The Owl Who Was Afraid of the Dark*. Puffin
Vipont, E. (1969) *The Elephant and the Bad Baby*. Hamish Hamilton
Wagner, J. (1977) *John Brown, Rose and the Midnight Cat*. Picture Puffin
Walker, B.K. (1975) *Teeny Tiny and the Witch Woman*. Puffin
Wolff, M. (1979) *Me In Puddles*. Abelard
Worthington, P. and S. (1981) *Teddy Bear Postman*. Puffin

Books about Reading and Language

Anderson, A.B. and Stokes, S.J. (1984) 'Social and Institutional Influences on the Development and Practice of Literacy', in Goelman, H. *et al.* (eds) *Awakening to Literacy*
Applebee, A.N. (1978) *The Child's Concept of Story*. University of Chicago Press
Bennett, J. (1979) *Learning to Read with Picture Books*. Signal Press
Bernstein, B. (1970) 'A Critique of the Concept of Compensatory Education', in Rubenstein and Stoneman (eds) *Education for Democracy*. Penguin
Bettelheim, B. (1978) *The Uses of Enchantment*. Penguin
Bloom, W. (1987) *Partnership with Parents in Reading*. Hodder & Stoughton
Brewer, W.F. (1985) 'The Story Schema: Universal and Culture-Specific Properties', in Olsen, D. *et al.* (eds) *Literacy, Language and Learning*. Cambridge University Press
Brice Heath, S. (1980) 'The Functions and Uses of Literacy', *Journal of Communication*, Winter
Brice Heath, S. (1982) 'What No Bedtime Story Means: Narrative Skills at Home and School', *Language and Society*, vol. 11
Brice Heath, S. (1983) *Ways With Words*. Cambridge University Press
Brice Heath, S. with Thomas, C. (1984) 'The Achievement of Pre-School Literacy for Mother and Child', in Goelman, H. *et al.* (eds) *Awakening to Literacy*
Britton, J. (1970) *Language and Learning*. Penguin
Britton, J. (1987) 'Vygotsky's Contribution to Pedagogical Theory', *English in Education*, vol. 21, no. 3
Bruner, J. (1978) 'The Role of Dialogue in Language Acquisition', in Sinclair, A., Jarvella, R.J. and Levelt, W.J.M. (eds) *The Child's Conception of Language*. Berlin: Springer-Verlag
Bruner, J. (1985) 'Vygotsky: a Historical and Conceptual Perspective', in Wertsch, J.V. (ed.) *Culture, Communication and Cognition*
Bruner, J. (1986) *Actual Minds, Possible Worlds*. Harvard University Press

Clark, M. (1976) *Young Fluent Readers*. Heinemann Educational

Cochran-Smith, M. (1986) 'Reading to Children: A Model for Understanding Texts', in Schieffelin, B. *et al.* (eds) *The Acquisition of Literacy*

Cook, E. (1969) *The Ordinary and the Fabulous*. Cambridge University Press

Cook-Gumperz, J. (1986) *The Social Construction of Literacy*. Cambridge University Press

Davies, M.M. (1989) *Television is Good for Your Kids*. Hilary Shipman

Department of Education and Science (1989) *English in the National Curriculum*. Her Majesty's Stationery Office

Docherty, M. (1984) 'That's Not Right. Look. There's No Daddy in this Book', in J. Miller (ed.) *Eccentric Propositions*. Routledge & Kegan Paul

Dombey, H. (1988) 'Partners in the Telling', in Meek, M. *et al.* (eds) *Language and Literacy in the Primary School*

Donaldson, M. (1978) *Children's Minds*. Fontana

Downing, J. (1969) 'How Children Think About Reading', *The Reading Teacher*, vol. 23 (iii)

Eliot, G. (reprinted 1977) 'Janet's Repentance', in *Scenes of Clerical Life*. Penguin

Forman, E.A. and Cazden, C.B. (1985) 'Exploring Vygotskian Perspectives in Education: The Cognitive Value of Peer Interaction', in Wertsch, J.V. (ed.) *Culture, Communication and Cognition*

Fox, C. (1983) 'Talking Like a Book: Young Children's Oral Monologues', in Meek, M. (ed.) *Opening Moves*. Bedford Way Papers 17, Institute of Education, University of London

Fry, D. (1985) *Children Talk About Books: Seeing Themselves as Readers*. Open University Press

Goelman, H., Oberg, A. and Smith, F. (eds) (1984) *Awakening to Literacy*. Heinemann Educational

Goodman, K. (1972) *Language and Literacy: the collected writings of Kenneth S. Goodman*, vols 1 and 2, Gollasch, F. (ed.) Routledge & Kegan Paul

Gregory, R.L. (1977) 'Ways Forward for the Psychologist: alternative fictions', in Meek, M. *et al.* (eds) *The Cool Web*

Harding, D.W. (1937) 'The Role of the Onlooker', *Scrutiny* VI (3). Deighton Bell, Cambridge

Harding, D.W. (1967) 'Considered Experience', *English in Education*, vol. 1, no. 2

Holdaway, D. (1979) *The Foundations of Literacy*. Ashton Scholastic

Iser, W. (1978) *The Act of Reading*. Johns Hopkins University Press

Jackson, B. (1979) *Starting School*. Croom Helm

Levine, K. (1986) *The Social Context of Literacy*. Routledge & Kegan Paul

Lightfoot, M. and Martin, N. (1988) *The Word for Teaching is Learning. Essays for James Britton*. Heinemann Educational

Maharaj Charan Singh (1966) *The Master Answers*. Radha Soami Satsang Beas, Punkab, India

Meek, M., Warlow, A. and Barton, G. (eds) (1977) *The Cool Web*. The Bodley Head

Meek, M. (1982) *Learning to Read*. The Bodley Head

Meek, M. (1986) 'Emergent Literacies: a Site for Analysis', *Language Arts*, Autumn 1

Meek, M. (1988) *How Texts Teach What Children Learn*. The Thimble Press

Meek, M. and Mills, C. (eds) (1988) *Language and Literacy in the Primary School*. The Falmer Press

Mills & Boon Ltd Romance Series

Minns, H. (1987) *From Home to School: Learning to Read*. MA Dissertation (unpublished), Institute of Education, University of London

Moon, C. (ed.) (1985) *Practical Ways to Teach Reading*. Ward Lock Educational

Moon, C. (1988) 'Reading: Where Are We Now?', in Meek, M. and Mills, C. (eds) *Language and Literacy in the Primary School*

Ninio, A. and Bruner, J. 'The Achievement and Antecedents of Labelling', *Child Language*, vol. 5

Reid, J. (1966) 'Learning to Think About Reading', *Educational Research*, vol. 9, no. 1

Rosen, C. and Rosen, H. (1973) *The Language of Primary School Children*. Penguin Education

Rosen, H. (1984) *Stories and Meanings*. National Association for the Teaching of English Papers in Education

Sartre, J.-P. (1964) *Words*. Penguin

Scollon, R. and Scollon, S. (1981) *Narrative, Literacy and Face in Interethnic Communication*. Ablex Publishing Corporation

Schieffelin, B. and Gilmore, P. (eds) (1986) *The Acquisition of Literacy: Ethnographic Perspectives*, vol. xxi. Ablex Publishing Corporation

Scribner, S. and Cole, M. (1981) *The Psychology of Literacy*. Harvard University Press

Simons, H.D. and Murphy, S. (1986) 'Spoken Language Strategies and Reading Acquisition', in Cook-Gumperz (ed.) *The Social Construction of Literacy*

Smith, F. (1971) *Understanding Reading*. Holt, Rinehart & Winston

Smith, F. (1973) *Psycholinguistics and Reading*. Holt, Rinehart & Winston

Smith, F. (1978) *Reading*. Cambridge University Press

Smith, F. (1984) *Essays into Literacy*. Heinemann Educational

Somerfield, M., Torbe, M. and Ward, C. (1983) *A Framework for Reading*. Heinemann Educational

Spencer, M. (1975) 'Learning to Read and the Reading Process', in Rosen, H. (ed.) *Language and Literacy in Our Schools*. Institute of Education, University of London

Spencer, M. (1976) 'Stories Are For Telling', *English in Education*, vol. 10, no. 1

Spencer, M. (1980) *Teaching Reading*, lecture delivered to Coventry branch of NATE

Spencer, M. (1980) 'Handing Down the Magic', in Salmon, P. (ed.) *Coming to Know*. Routledge & Kegan Paul

Street, B. (1984) *Literacy in Theory and Practice*. Cambridge University Press

Tansley, A.E. (1967) *Reading and Remedial Reading*. Routledge & Kegan Paul

Taylor, D. (1983) *Family Literacy*. Heinemann Educational

Teale, W.H. (1984) 'Reading to Young Children: its Significance for Literacy Development', in Goelman, H. *et al.* (eds) *Awakening to Literacy*

Tizard, B. and Hughes, M. (1984) *Young Children Learning*. Fontana

Torbe, M. (1980) *Reader, Book and World*, lecture delivered to Coventry branch of NATE

Vygotsky, L. (1978) *Mind in Society*, ed. Cole, M. *et al.* Harvard University Press

Wade, B. 'Story at Home and School,' *Educational Review* Occasional Paper No. 10

Walker, A. (1983) *The Color Purple*. The Women's Press

Waterland, L. (1988) *Read With Me*. The Thimble Press

Weir, R. (1962) *Language in the Crib*. Janua Linguarum Series Maior 14. The Hague: Mouton & Co.

Wells, G. (1981) *Learning Through Interaction*. Cambridge University Press

Wells, G. (1985) *Language, Learning and Education*. NFER-Nelson

Wells, G. (1987) *The Meaning Makers*. Hodder & Stoughton

Wertsch, J.V. (ed.) (1985) *Culture, Communication and Cognition*. Cambridge University Press

Widlake, P. and Macleod, F. (1984) *Raising Standards*. Coventry: Community Education Development Centre

Index

THE EDUCATION SERIES
In association with the University of London Institute of Education
Series Editor JANE MILLER

In recent years the attacks on education in Britain have meant a complete redrawing of the educational map. But attempts to stifle opposition and resistance have neither silenced nor deterred those who are doing innovatory work in every aspect of the field. In support of this radical tradition, Virago has launched a new education series, published in association with the University of London Institute of Education, committed to providing information and understanding of the social, cultural and developmental issues of significance in education today. It presents some of the most exciting and important thinking in ways which will appeal to professionals as well as to students and parents and all those for whom education is a central and continuing concern. The books are by teachers and researchers and originate from classrooms in schools and colleges, from the practices of teaching and the experiences of learning. The series' general editor is Jane Miller, Senior Lecturer in the Joint Department of English and Media Studies at the Institute of Education.

UN/POPULAR FICTIONS

Gemma Moss

Many young people take popular fiction as the model for their own writing. Yet little has been done to account for the preponderance of such forms or the function they fulfil for their writers. Concentrating on girls' use of romance, Gemma Moss shows that they are not mindlessly enslaved to the forms they reproduce, but are actively deploying them to raise rich and complex questions about social identity. She suggests that by drawing attention to the contradictions between the different sets of knowledge children use in their writing, questions about power and questions about difference, about masculinity and femininity can be raised. *Un/Popular Fictions* examines the conflicting assumptions made about the role of texts in the social development of children, suggests new strategies for classroom teaching, and offers new insights into the ways in which cultural identities are negotiated.

TEACHING BLACK LITERATURE

Suzanne Scafe

In examining the role of literature in a multicultural curriculum Suzanne Scafe challenges the literary tradition in education and the criteria by which texts enter that tradition. She argues for the urgent need to review the early initiatives within the education system which prompted the change from a monocultural approach to teaching to a multicultural approach, and discusses how these strategies for change are flawed: for example, it is not enough to introduce a few Black texts in what is little more than a tokenistic gesture. This becomes, for Black students, an experience of being patronised by the school, the curriculum and the teachers. Suzanne Scafe stresses how crucial the task is for educationalists to ensure that Black writing is valued critically: that it is read, both as a cultural and artistic whole and as a reflection of the political and cultural struggles which give it its context.

COUNTING GIRLS OUT
Girls and Mathematics Unit, Institute of Education

Compiled by Valerie Walkerdine

The question of girls' attainment in mathematics is met with every kind of myth, false 'evidence', and theorising about the gendered body and the gendered mind. The Girls and Mathematics Unit has, over a period of ten years, carried out detailed theoretical and empirical investigations in this area. In taking issue with truisms such as: women are irrational, illogical and too close to their emotions to be any good at mathematics, this study examines and puts into historical perspective claims made about women's minds. It analyses the relationship between evidence and explanation: why are girls still taken to be lacking when they perform well, and boys taken to possess something even when they perform poorly? *Counting Girls Out* is an enquiry into the bases of these assumptions; it contains examples of work carried out with girls, their teachers and their families – at home and in the classroom – and discusses the problems and possibilities of feminist research more generally.

WASTING GIRLS' TIME
The Problem of Home Economics

Dena Attar

Wasting Girls' Time, a critical examination of the history and current status of domestic subjects in schools, looks at why and how these subjects were first included in school curricula, their subsequent effect on girls' education as a whole, and what feminist opposition to them has been. It also focuses on the struggles of domestic science pioneers and their modern counterparts to defend, upgrade and modernise their subject in spite of their low status, and the subject's identity as the domain of girls and women. It explores where boys fit in, what courses they are offered, how their attitudes differ and whether domestic subjects should be taught to both sexes. Using contemporary teaching materials, syllabuses and classroom observations, this informative study provides a detailed picture of home economics in schools now, and questions whether this subject has had its day or not.

Other Virago Books of Interest

DEMOCRACY IN THE KITCHEN
Regulating Mothers and Socialising Daughters

Valerie Walkerdine and Helen Lucey

How are daughters raised, how are mothers made to be 'proper' mothers, and what does all this have to do with democracy? From the post-war period, with its emphasis on expanding educational possibilities for all children, to equal opportunities in the 1970s and '80s, the prevailing notion has been that 'natural' mothering (for how could it be otherwise?) would produce 'normal' children, fit for the new democratic age. These ideas have become commonsense ones, but at what cost to the lives of women? Valerie Walkerdine and Helen Lucey explore these effects by examining a well-known study of four-year-olds with their mothers, and in doing so, they tell us a different story about the divides of class and gender and the consequent social inequalities. The authors argue that although ideas from developmental psychology are held to be progressive, they serve to support the view that there is something wrong with working-class mothering which could be put right by making it more middle-class. But nor is the middle-class home one of happy normality: in both classes, women are differently, but oppressively, regulated. In this provocative book, the authors call for a new feminist engagement with class and gender socialisation to constitute a new politics of difference.

THE TIDY HOUSE
Little Girls' Writing

Carolyn Steedman

Three working-class eight-year-old girls write a story, 'The Tidy House'. It is about the house they will live in one day, the streets of their own decaying urban estate, about love and motherhood and the pattern of life they expect to inherit. The children in the story are themselves as they believe their parents see them – longed for, yet because of poverty, also sources of irritation and resentment.

In analysing this fascinating document, the author uses her remarkable perceptions of children's writing and their expectations of the world, as well as literature, linguistics, theories of education and history, to come to her highly original and controversial conclusions on how children confront the way things are and imagine the way things might be.

'. . . very interesting and heartening. Seeing the problems and rewards of children's perceptions and writings that close is a great help to understanding a much wider and more persistent process' – *Raymond Williams*

'. . . a revelation – superbly constructed and illuminating. Opens up new ways of looking at the way children learn' – *Dale Spender*